THE UNDYING SOUL

THE
UNDYING
SOUL

A Cancer Doctor's Discovery

STEPHEN J. IACOBONI, MD

PUBLISHED BY STEPHEN J. IACOBONI, MD
WWW.THEUNDYINGSOUL.COM

SJI
PUBLISHING

First Edition

ISBN:
978-0-9830538-0-4

Published by Stephen J. Iacoboni, MD PA
SJI Publishng
Kennewick, Washington
www.theundyingsoul.com

Dedication

To my mother, Gloria N. Iacoboni,
who said these words to me as she lay dying of cancer,

"You are so beautiful..."

Contents

Acknowledgments

⁓

BECAUSE I AM NOT A PROFESSIONAL WRITER, it took me many years of research and countless drafts to complete this book. During that time I received assistance from friends and colleagues, readers, and a number of editors, all of whom helped me along the way. I would in particular like to thank Marty Staley and Kathy Bowlin, both for reads and manuscript preparation; Mary Langer Smith, who patiently and generously guided me past so many obstacles; and finally my very dear friend, Seth Norman, himself one of the best writers alive today, for suggestions that helped me to clarify ideas, express the passions I feel, and which I hope make these stories more enjoyable to read.

I must also thank my former wife, Mary, for allowing me to retire to my study so many weekend nights, to plug away at this for almost a decade. Lord knows (and so does Mary) how consuming a doctor's life can be, even more so when he quests to understand mysteries. To that I would add my appreciation for our fine sons Michael and Gabriel, with special thank to Christopher, who did such an outstanding job as copy editor.

At last…while I cannot name the many, many patients who provided the very inspiration of this book, they deserve my greatest appreciation for teaching me such astonishing lessons. I hope and trust they know the depth of my devotion, and will accept the gratitude expressed on these pages.

Thank you.

Stephen J. Iacoboni, MD

A Preface

FOR READERS WHO DON'T READ PREFACES, PROLOGUES OR INTRODUCTIONS

I'M WITH YOU. But hoping you'll try this time, I'll keep this brief.

Where we all came from is a great mystery. But to where we return is the secret that most concerns, intrigues and terrifies the cancer patients I have treated every single day of my life as a clinical oncologist.

Twenty-eight years, over 5000 patients: you might expect that I have seen miraculous recoveries. I have.

You may presume I have witnessed many thousands of deaths. Sadly, that's so.

What you might not imagine, however, is that I have also experienced *miraculous deaths*—events I never expected, shared with me by extraordinary people. These extraordinary events were personally life changing, because they illuminated concepts I could not possibly contemplate when I started out as a doctor. In those early days of my career, I was so dedicated to *science* that I dismissed any other approach to understanding life.

Miracles changed me. As a young man I had been taught to consider life, disease and death as marvelous but merely complex organic processes: facts and phenomena to observe and influence. I regarded these as no more mystical, given time and proper instruments, than algebra. But I grew into a doctor humbled by the generosity and passionate spirit of my patients, enlightened by those who allowed me to understand "life with cancer" and "death by cancer" in entirely new ways.

This took time, and many lessons. A great deal of time; many, many lessons—the kind of depth and breadth of experience offered to, and imposed upon, a doctor treating a fierce illness too often lethal. Even as a soldier fighting individual battles in our ongoing "war against cancer"—a disease that kills more people than all wars put together—the revelations came oh-so-slowly. And, often, oh-so-painfully, as you would guess and I confess.

But not fought for naught. Now, thanks to those patients who've lived and died, I find myself able to do so much more for the precious people I now treat, and will treat in the future.

My patients' stories provide the substance of this book. To these I will add the commentary I can, building from insights, synthesizing when I think I must. Forgive me if what I say seems at times incredible to you. It certainly was to me, at the time. I am truly sorry that I cannot promise you an easy journey. However, what I do promise are eventual triumphs, and my *hope* is that you will find each step valuable, each patient a teacher. I'll tell you right now that I think of many of my patients as "angels."

And I hope that their lessons will provide you with ideas to ponder, which, taken *together,* will ultimately offer you the sustaining vision gifted to me.

That's important. Well beyond, in fact, any worldly importance to me, for it is my belief that they reveal what I choose to call, carefully but with conviction, *The Undying Soul.*

Chapter One

⟲

THE LONELY VIGIL

Huddled together in an unfamiliar hospital room, loving family members and friends sit at the bedside of the dying cancer patient. Hours turn into days, or longer. *It's only a matter of time,* we hear, think, and sometimes say. But what kind of *time* is this? Isolated from the vibrancy of life just outside the hospital room, it's difficult to escape feelings of bewilderment and isolation. Exactly how do we quantify measures of loneliness and fear?

A matter of time provides small consolation to someone fighting for each breath, or to those watching death take someone they love. But during that wait the most ancient of questions visit both patient and watchers: Is there life after death? What's next—for me, you, us? What, *what*…is really happening now?

Take a step back and you might wonder why, after a lifetime, these issues seem at this moment so sudden and so strange. You may ask yourself why stories and assumptions we've accepted so long—explanations of death, promises, assurances—all feel so ephemeral, just when we need them the most.

This much I can tell you from experience: for many of my patients, part of this dilemma results from an unspoken conspiracy of silence. People do not want to talk about imminent death in modern Western culture, save possibly with a few trusted family members or friends.

Even then, we often stick to practical matters or heartfelt farewells. If we are able, we express love and pride, grief or regrets—but talk about *death*? To speak of death itself?

To whom can we talk about overwhelming doubts and apprehensions? To whom can we describe the sense of this great unknown approaching closer, but never defined by conscious light? Even if we could frame these thoughts and emotions, who would listen and could bear to hear?

Me. I listen. I have done so with thousands of patients over three decades. I write this book to share with you what I've heard, what I have learned, what I've come to believe and, honestly, hope you will believe too. Too often we speak of death as a "last frontier" even while living our lives as if we will never go there. What's obvious to the intellect is unbearable to our emotional selves.

Some say death is the reason people developed religion; and for millennia, religion has given us answers. But in an increasingly secular world, religion's answers seemingly fall to whispers, or fail us altogether.

Count me as one of those for whom this failure was a reality for a very long time. How long? Until I found it almost unbearable. Until the urgency I saw and felt in my patients' eyes all but overwhelmed me. To a point where a part of me deep within, untouched by my professional detachment, forced me to contemplate those ancient questions with something like the immediacy manifest by my dying patients and their loved ones...to ask, in advance of my own demise, *what* is happening here?

Asking is one thing. But the answer to "How long?" was simply this: *Until at last I made the discovery that allowed me to believe differently.*

After years of addressing the physical needs of my cancer patients with CAT scans and chemotherapy, I eventually became more and more concerned with something less obvious than the gross symptoms of cellular carnage.

That *something* is as ancient as our time on earth, as immediate as "only a matter of," and in special moments, became as obvious to me as any empirical fact published in scientific journals...

...*Soul.*

You may understand that this subject is among the most dangerous of all for a doctor of our time. I certainly do. For most of my career I considered the issue completely irrelevant. Listening to whatever a patient believed and wanted to share; that's one thing. But discussing a concept like *soul* was unthinkable. Offering opinions or challenging a patient's beliefs...was misguided and presumptuous; and, of course, as professionally perilous as a malpractice charge. But again...I wasn't even tempted. In fact, if I would not have carried a pitchfork in a mob determined to confront such an heretical MD, I would have at least lit one of the torches. And for years after that, during a period of doubt, I would have still held back in the shadows.

Oddly and ironically, I began to surrender that attitude—slowly, reluctantly, at my patients' insistence—for the same reasons I became a doctor: to relieve suffering, to nurture, to heal. Patients taught me that our current approach to the cancer "experience" breaks hearts and leaves people spiritually bereft; that while cancer itself may be physically dev-astating, it is our neglect of the spiritual and emotional manifestations arising from this disease that prevent us from glimpsing something of vital importance.

And that something, I will tell you now—the thing I hope to prove to you over a few hundred pages—is the true existence of what I call *The Undying Soul.*

I don't imagine that will be an easy task. Certainly not for people as "science-centric" as I was for most of my life, and perhaps not for those whose convictions are prescribed by one religion or another. But believe me when I promise you that this a journey worth taking.

Slowly. I ask for your patience, and will begin by trying to win your trust.

Also ironically, I will establish that trust, I hope, even as I erode one of the foundations on which you might build it.

Chapter Two

⟿

PROMISES, PROMISES

IN JULY OF 1982 I entered my medical oncology fellowship at MD Anderson Cancer Center, in Houston, Texas. I begin this book with that acknowledgment for three reasons.

First: MD Anderson was then and remains today a world-renowned, university-based teaching hospital, one of the premier cancer research facilities in the world. By that I mean to imply—really, I just want you to know—that I began my career in this specialty by training at the upper echelon, a new doctor on the cutting edge of contemporary research and practice.

I belonged at Anderson—philosophically, I mean. As a young, atheist intellectual, fresh out of med school and full of hubris, I chose oncology because I wanted to prove that science and logic could triumph over *anything*—even cancer. If I had issues with that great institution—and I did, as you will see—none of these resulted from spiritual or religious issues. Quite the contrary: although raised in an ancient faith, I had lapsed completely, embracing instead the reigning dogma of scientific method and a seemingly benign, essentially existential commitment to *making people well* through the interventions of researchers and doctors like the one I hoped to become. Empirical evidence, responsible experiments, "better living through chemistry"—I saluted everything I thought "M.D." and MD Anderson stood for.

The second reason, extrapolated from the first, was that in many ways, my oncology *alma mater* represents conventional cancer treatment then, and still does now more often than not. The chemistry changes, wonderfully; so do surgical techniques and marvelous radiation technologies.

I'll speak more to that, but before I do, let me introduce my third reason: Leslie. That wasn't her real name, but it will do. She was a very real thirty-six-year-old white female, wife to Alan, mother of two, admitted to the breast cancer ward on the first day of my first Anderson rotation.

Leslie was special for all kinds of reasons. The least of these, however, was important to me: Leslie was my first patient as a medical oncology fellow-in-training.

We talked for hours. I can still remember my feelings during these early conversations, each one brilliant with hope. For her, hope of life.

For me...finally! After so many years of school and training, caring for Leslie would give meaning to all those years of hard work and preparation. Our special bond was forged by mutual purpose and our ferocious dedication to a single goal: *her survival.*

I live for this, I thought back then. And I suppose I thought every variation on that theme—this is why I live, to serve, to protect, to heal.

I live for this.

But Leslie did not. She will die for you in a few pages, as she died for Alan and her children, her family, friends, and me almost three decades ago. She did not know that would happen when she arrived. Neither did those who would lose her; nor did I, I would like to say for the record, and for what it's worth.

And that's the issue here: What *should* Leslie have known? What should I, her doctor, have understood *and acknowledged*...to her, to Alan and her family?

Those questions are as alive today as they were back then. To address them, to begin a long process, I must start with MD Anderson itself, less as an institution I still greatly admire than as an icon. Because the *expectation* of cure is what Anderson offered and intended to provide—however unlikely the odds.

A more formal introduction: The MD Anderson Cancer Center stands twelve stories high, an immense building occupying a full city block. Its exterior walls are faced by a rare pink granite. Solid, imposing—the stone provides sharp contrast to the surrounding glass-windowed skyscrapers, flashy but fragile, built by and for the oil industry of the Gulf. There is no mistaking that contrast and its meaning. MD Anderson is a fortress, a "cancer castle" complete with separate towers for the transplant facilities. I expect it was the architect's intention, to conjure the sense of security and protection this building promotes in so many who see it, to ensure the certainty that within this edifice they will find strength…and more.

Certainly that's the hope of the patients occupying Anderson's 1200 beds and also the mission of the hospital's 400-person medical staff. Among them you will find world experts in every branch of cancer medicine. They are the elite. If the hospital's a castle, its staff are crusaders on a quest, determined to effect the impossible: to defeat the most frightening of modern-day medical demons. They are knights and wizards attempting that most difficult of exorcisms…

Most aptly, an order of true alchemists; if I was new to oncology then, the specialty itself was still in its infancy, full of optimism, flush with the excitement created by "the biochemical revolution" that had unraveled the mystery of DNA, the chemical basis of life itself. Biological science taught us that cancer was just a cellular abnormality that could be cured biochemically—magical molecules were all we needed! We weren't interested in "wasting time" worrying about anything beyond our patients' physiology and anatomy; we dealt mainly in experimental drugs that would beat this disease in the end. Astronauts right there in Houston had just "conquered" space; from where we stood on our own frontier, it was *obvious* that a breakthrough curative treatment was imminent, soon to be revealed by our investigations.

That confidence created an aura recognized around the world—by wealthy Texans, of course; by Americans across the country; also by Middle Eastern sheiks, Venezuelan oil barons and Asian tycoons. The word was out: "If you don't want to die, go to Houston."

That was the word, and it truly inspired those who had the will and the means. Being a state university hospital, Anderson was readily accessible to Texas residents. Out-of-state referral admissions were also available, and Anderson became a beacon of hope to our clientele: determined and committed people, typically with highly supportive families —patients who urgently needed our help and *also* had the energy and resources to make a long journey.

This also meant that, more often than not, these folks brought with them an unrealistic expectation. They came to MD Anderson for a *cure*, even though almost all had already been told by their doctor at home that no known cure existed. They journeyed from all over the country and all over the world, making special, often extraordinary efforts, specifically to yield themselves to MD Anderson's entrancement.

Confidence and promise drove us. All of us—doctors and patients alike—had somehow failed to get the message, already delivered time after time: *most cancers were incurable.*

As to the souls of those who came with hope, and died without any…not an issue. Not science. Not our job.

That brings me back to Leslie. Alan and their children were at her bedside when I first entered her hospital room. From her medical history I knew that two years before her hometown surgeon had removed her left breast, which contained a two-inch malignant tumor. Unfortunately, he'd also found that the cancer had already spread to the lymph nodes under her armpit.

Her surgeon back home had given Leslie post-operative chemotherapy, although not in the recommended levels we use today. This was not itself unusual: during the early '80s, surgeons provided much of the oncology treatment in many smaller communities.

That chemo failed. Leslie's cancer reappeared, now in her lungs and liver. The surgeon told her there was nothing more he could do.

That brought Leslie to MD Anderson. Like all patients, she hoped to live. Like most who came this far, she expected she would, given our care. And, confidently, we encouraged her expectation, *however unlikely the odds.*

An Environment of Optimism—and the Truth

If our optimism created a worldwide aura, that's partly because the air of denial within our famous center was thicker than the pink stone walls. The truth—the facts as I learned them over time—presented a picture less rosy. Among these: our arsenal for fighting cancer at the time consisted of only a handful of partially effective chemotherapeutic agents. The side effects of these medications were frankly horrendous. It wasn't unusual for patients to be violently ill for three days following each chemotherapy treatment.

Add these together and what frequently happened was this: patients suffered from the cancer *and* the chemotherapy…and then they died.

We, the doctors, understood this. But *you* wouldn't, by looking at us or listening to what we said. We wore long white lab coats with the brightly colored insignia of our institution on our shoulders, our chests emblazoned with our embroidered names, followed by the sacrosanct initials "M.D." We understood but refused to accept the existing limitations of the prevailing "state of the art." We were on a mission: to us was entrusted the noble goal of finding a cure for cancer. To that end we were empowered to put into experimental use the most potent "investigational" pharmaceuticals on the planet. If these were not powerful enough—and they weren't—to us fell the task of testing new formulations that might eventually prove themselves in our relentlessly ongoing research.

Might prove. We were…testing. With the experiments of these drugs on animals complete by the time they came into our hands…*we* began on people. Human research: our job—my job, I would realize—was to experiment with promising *new* chemotherapies by administering them to otherwise-incurable cancer patients. By this process, and only by such processes, might we realize the breakthroughs that Science promised, and thus improve upon the admittedly limited armamentarium described above.

No one denied that this was our purpose. Nobody lied to patients. We didn't need to. Instead, we built an institutional denial into a modus operandi, using protocols I learned and followed…

…Starting with Leslie.

Hospital rooms for new patients are often crowded with anxious family members, all intent on every word and gesture that passes between doctor and patient. This is especially true during the initial encounter. Leslie herself was demure, thoughtful and nervous; she and her children, parents and husband listened carefully to what I had to say—a description of her condition as things stood, and the options we would consider.

Then they waited. Surely there was something *else* I would tell them?

Of course, and I realized it was this: *They wanted me to promise a cure.*

How I wished I could. The problem was simple: *I knew of no cure.* In no case I had read of in the literature or discussed in my medical training had anybody with her condition ever survived.

That's not what I told Leslie and those who loved her. Instead, I followed protocol, explaining that I was a fellow, in training, under close supervision. I would present her case to my professor, and return with a plan of action.

What happened after that was standard practice, I would discover over the course of three years, almost regardless of a patient's condition. I reported Leslie's case as I found it, but the results were the same with others even more extreme: "Mrs. 'Parker' has widespread metastatic uterine cancer," I would tell my professor. "She received all of the standard chemotherapies from her local oncologist in Peoria. She's forty-five years old, married and the mother of three children in high school. In my preliminary discussion with the patient and her husband I tried to tell her that her situation was not promising...do you have any special recommendations I can bring back to Mrs. Parker and her family?"

Almost invariably, my professor's answer would go like this: "That doesn't sound too bad. She's otherwise in pretty good shape. Let's try her on one of our experimental protocols. Maybe she'll get a good response."

And that, almost verbatim, is what my professor told Leslie and her husband. He understood their expectations, and accepted these; he also told them that every patient who checks into the Cancer Center is eligible for a cure, and that the mission of the Institute was to find this cure and administer it. No detailed discussion about limitations or long odds...

In those days I was known by my peers as an idealist, which is why I belonged philosophically at MD Anderson; I too shared the institute's passion to fulfill that noble and ideal goal of discovering the cure for cancer. But I was also realistic, so this protocol troubled me. And yet, I was in fact a new trainee, in no position to question the authority of a more experienced supervisor. All I could do was hope he was right.

I carried out my orders and treated Leslie according to the prevailing investigational protocol. I found hope and fought doubts: maybe she *could* be cured by the new concoction—who was I to say otherwise?

Who indeed? But I struggled with myself as I scrolled through the master protocol manual, realizing that for patients like Leslie there had been new medical regimens put to the test every two months for the past three years.

Why this continual stream of new regimens? What were the outcomes from these "potentially curative" treatments not found worthy for continued investigation? Failure. Sadly, hundreds of patients had achieved no more than little response or tumor shrinkage. One by one, each protocol followed a predecessor into research oblivion.

Why, I wondered, should I expect that this time things would be different? And…why should Leslie? Leslie and her husband had come to MD Anderson with great expectations. After listening to my professor and interpreting what he said *and did not say,* they now expected only one thing from me: a cure.

And by God—by Science, I mean (remember, I was a staunch atheist at the time)—that's what I set out to deliver. It was for me as T.S. Eliot wrote in *East Coker:* "For us there is only the trying. The rest is not our business."

Try we did. Our search for a cure began with aggressive chemotherapy that caused Leslie's hair to fall out and diminished her ability to taste, smell, and hold a pencil. The new regimen also destroyed her nerve tissue, which would not, ever, regenerate. Some of the tumors in Leslie's lungs and liver actually did get smaller…

What they did *not* do, however, was disappear.

To my mind these were insufficient results, given how weakened the chemo left Leslie. Still, she and Alan were keen to fight on. And so we did. As often happened when the first treatment regimen failed to eradicate cancer, Leslie was assigned to the succeeding protocol. I expected that. What I did not expect was that my supervising professor's next conversation with Leslie and her husband would sound so much like the first—so similar that it left me incredulous.

According to him, Leslie had done very *well* with her first treatment, but some of the cancer remained. She needed a new approach to kill off the cancer cells that were "apparently resistant to the first set of drugs."

While that explanation appears plausible, every first-year medical student learns that human physiology is far more complicated than this makes it seem. Existing research revealed a more likely outcome. The cancer cells in Leslie's liver and lungs that survived the first round of chemotherapy would probably survive anything else we threw at them.

I knew that. But so did my professor, and he had not deemed it necessary to convey this information; and that constrained me. Perhaps he hesitated to convey pessimism, guessing—correctly, I think—that Leslie and Alan wanted only reason to hope.

And there is still hope, I reminded myself, trying not to add the caveat *though precious little.*

I had to remind myself often. Leslie, Alan and I met every single day except for the two Sundays per month I had off. Our visits were filled with the intensity, apprehension and drama that unavoidably defines Leslie's predicament. My primary role in her care was to ameliorate the chemotherapy-induced side effects. Every day we discussed her nausea, loss of appetite, pain, anxiety, sleep disturbance, and depression.

We also talked about her hopes and her expectations. "Boy, I can't wait for the chemo to work so we can go home," Leslie said once. "Molly starts soccer practice soon and I've got to get back to work." I never squelched these dreams, but I could see her dying slowly before my eyes. Subtle signs: etched lines above her eyebrow, her panting breaths as she walked to the commode, a hesitation in each step....

Nobody else noticed—or no one would admit it. Not my professor, and certainly not Leslie or Alan, who were only too eager to talk about the new super-chemo compounds that would soon eliminate the uncontrollable growth of her cancer cells. *Uncontrollable.* That's what they were…that's what they remained.

In the following weeks Leslie, Alan and I never managed a truly objective discussion about her condition. By that I mean we never mentioned the "possibility"—in fact, the overwhelming likelihood—that she would die from this disease. Despite my frequent insinuations, Leslie and Alan always evaded any talk of failure. That was their choice. I respected that then, and now. But it was also my dilemma, and as Leslie continued to deteriorate the situation became ever more unbearable.

It was a Thursday evening when Leslie's nurse called me, just as I was heading home after a fourteen-hour workday. By then it had been ten hours since I'd examined her on my morning rounds. The nurse was detecting subtle changes: Leslie's eye movements were erratic, she seemed confused….

By the time I got to her room Leslie was incoherent. Her symptoms indicated the possibility of malignant meningitis—a thankfully rare, but particularly virulent and universally fatal form of her disease's progression.

There was only one way to know for certain: I performed a spinal tap on her myself at her bedside that evening, submitting the spinal fluid for test results that would not be back until morning. After the procedure, I spent another hour with Alan, reviewing over and over again all the "what-ifs."

Almost all.

The next morning began one of those summer days in Houston when walking from the parking lot to the hospital entrance threatened hyperthermia and dehydration. Even so, I suspected much of the sweat staining my shirt was prompted by anxiety for Leslie and what I would learn when I opened her chart. I hoped my fear was unwarranted, not because I had faith that the news might be good, but because at that moment I couldn't grasp how Alan and their children would cope with such a tragic loss. This was an event for which they still seemed to me to be completely *unprepared*.

For that matter, how would *I* cope?

When I entered her room Leslie was looking and feeling better—and could say so. This put Alan at ease but worried me even more. If she did have malignant meningitis, the steroids I'd administered the night before would give her just this relief—but only for a very short period of time. It's so deceiving, an Indian summer of hours before a winter of—

Worry doesn't always prepare you for the worst. Not me, anyway. I read the lab results from Leslie's spinal fluid tap with horror and sadness. No doubt about it: Leslie's cancer had spread to her meninges, the spinal cord. She would surely die now, and there was nothing I could do about it.

What does a fireman say to the mother of a child he cannot rescue? What does a highway patrolman say to a husband whose wife has just perished on the road, or a ship captain to his crew as they head into a typhoon? What could I say to Alan, after six weeks of an intimate relationship full of promises—*implicit* promises—that none of us at the hospital could now keep?

Nothing. I could say nothing that *mattered*.

Leslie lived for four days after developing her malignant meningitis. Her death was slow and wretched. Alan kept looking at me with sheer disbelief. I repeated to him, over and over, that there were no guarantees in the world of experimental medicine.

He couldn't hear me. He watched Leslie—gaunt, delirious, crippled, her skin as bare a newborn's, her body older like that of an ancient… Alan watched until, mercifully, Leslie gasped her last breath. Then he bent over her body sobbing, unable to face me.

I left him to his mourning. I came back soon, to try to console him. But he was gone.

I'm not sure whether Alan ever forgave me for losing his Leslie, because I never saw him again. I'd understand if he held me responsible. He knew that I understood his hope and expectations. No matter my insinuations, I had never told him:

"It's just a matter of time."

Chapter 3

⁓

SEARCHING BUT
NOT KNOWING

LESLIE...WAS NOT A MIRACLE. And I did warn you. I even apologized in advance.

But do know now, miracles *will* come. I promise. Meanwhile, about promises...

I arrived at MD Anderson determined to save patients' lives through clinical skill and scientific knowledge. Medical science then—and even now, twenty-eight years later—has not advanced enough to save patients like Leslie. As I suspected at the time, and would soon confirm for myself, bombarding desperately ill people with unproven and highly toxic chemo compounds rarely produces the desired effect.

Eventually I would object to this approach to treating cancer patients, after I fully understood that, however scientific our treatments, the offer of hope was mainly philosophic. We offered encouragement based not on the existing evidence, but on a faith that Science—unproven, experimental, theoretical, "what-if-we-try-this" science—would provide the answer. Someday. Somehow. To someone.

Thus we fueled their hopes, as well as our own. And we ran our protocols—"we," the division of Developmental Therapeutics. Our mission was to inject FDA-approved experimental compounds into our desperate and willing subjects, hoping for a fantastic, *heretofore-never-achieved* response. Unfortunately, "never-achieved" means the effects of such drugs on human beings were unknown; it was precisely those effects we were investigating.

To me, *unknown,* unproven and "heretofore-never-achieved" came to mean worrisome, potentially dangerous, "try-at-your-peril." To the optimistic patients and their desperate families, however, *unknown* translated into hope and possibility.

It never got easier. Leslie's story was the first of countless similar scenarios I witnessed. I tried to believe, and still do, that everyone at MD Anderson—professors, doctors, trainees, nurses and patients— were willing and heroic participants in a desperate, too often futile anti-cancer crusade, and that by their grit we advanced. But day after day there, then week after week, I witnessed one disappointing story after another. Expectations shattered, along with hopes and dreams, successive failures mounting amidst our never-ending search for "the cure."

In times of desperation I insisted to my professors—truly, some of the world's elite—that there must be a better way to deal with patients and their families, something more humane.

They would not listen. Their goal was research; their hope was for successes that must surely come some day if only they just kept trying. Meanwhile, trench warfare must continue: send another wave of brave young soldiers into no-man's land, assuming one day they'll break through. As physicians, we mainly discussed response rates, percentages of tumor shrinkage and severity of side effects. While successful "treatment outcomes" were rare—as in, "the patient lived" or got better— there remained the inexplicable expectation that success was—or *would be someday soon*—a commonplace occurrence.

Despite my criticisms, sometimes outspoken, my professors acknowledged my clinical skills by awarding me a coveted junior professorship. I accepted the position thinking that in this role I might at least modify MD Anderson's message, injecting a modicum of realism. I spoke more candidly than my peers, telling patients, "We'll do all that's humanly possible for you, but only time will tell whether our efforts prove successful. The outcomes in investigational therapeutics are, by definition, unknown, and are exactly what we're trying to determine with this research."

I thought this was honesty. A few patients—one too many—disagreed. They complained about "equivocations." They knew what they wanted and why they had come: to be cured. I heard many variations on the theme "Don't tell me 'maybe' or 'if.' Tell me *what* will work, and *when*." Often the undercurrent resembled that choice made by Leslie and Alan: *don't dash our hopes with reason.*

Meanwhile, there was no question that MD Anderson's professors were doing their best, battling the disease with every new regimen possible. But a *research* hospital is just that; despite good intentions, patients like Leslie all too often became statistics in the end.

And so my dilemma grew. This wasn't what I aspired to when I chose to become an oncologist. Whatever the justifications, I sensed that something vital was missing, always beyond my grasp. I began to wonder if there was not a factor left out of this data-driven paradigm, if there might be more to the human equation, a mystery unsolved in the balance between patients' life, and death and disease.

Never did we look for or try to save the soul of our patients. We were supposedly among the most brilliant medical investigators in the world, and yet we had no knowledge of or interest in that which mattered most.

Knowing something's absent doesn't amount to much, unless you look for it. I soon understood that I could not make any progress with my search in a hospital environment that to me alone felt so deadly.

As to a guide, I had none. But I did have a warning that would do for the moment.

Since medical school I had carried a black notebook in the breast pocket of my doctor's coat. Onto its cover—now a long succession of covers—I'd pasted a stanza from a sixteenth-century essay by John Donne. You've heard it, I know, and it captures the passion and humility I have felt every day as a cancer doctor:

> No man is an Island.
> Every man's death diminishes me.
> Therefore, do not send to know
> For whom the bell tolls.
> It tolls for thee.

A caution. Also a kind of promise.

Although my disillusionment at MD Anderson sowed the seeds of discontent toward my chosen profession, it took almost twenty years for me to realize what I was searching for. During all that time the recognition of cancer's true relationship to the undying human soul remained hidden from me. To find the answers, to fill the void, to make the discovery that is revealed in these pages, I needed to keep searching.

So twenty-five years ago, I set out to do just that.

I left my MD Anderson professorship behind and moved to the San Francisco Bay Area where I worked for one year in a large HMO. I then decided to start anew as the first medical oncologist to ever set up practice in the semi-rural town of Walla Walla, Washington (home of Bugs Bunny!). I remained there for sixteen years before I moved to beautiful Coeur d'Alene, Idaho, population 40,059. In a smaller town I thought I could be more honest with my patients and achieve a better emotional outcome, for them and for myself. The mystery of the undying soul and its relationship to cancer still lay hidden from me.

Chapter Four

~

THE HUMAN NEED

I'LL NEVER FORGET MY FIRST DAY in neuroanatomy class as a second year-medical student. Seated at our lab benches, each of us with a three-gallon plastic tub on the table, we listened to an introductory lecture, at last obeying instructions to open our containers and remove the specimen contained inside.

That "specimen" was an intact human brain floating in formaldehyde. For the next six weeks we carved up those brains like pumpkins, identifying and tracing the neuronal pathways and anatomical structures of that special organ that generates human consciousness.

This is just one of countless examples from my medical and basic science education that illustrate how I was thoroughly trained to regard the human being as an organic machine, and to see life as a magnificent "mechanism." Chemistry taught us that life arose spontaneously out of the inorganic realm of water, minerals, and gases. I was taught that the gap between the inorganic (nonliving) and the organic (living) is small, and that all living creatures, including *Homo sapiens*, are merely complex machines ultimately reducible to quantitative analysis.

To the cardiologist who places a Teflon stent in a partially blocked coronary artery, this concept poses no apparent dilemma. Nor is there any problem for the ophthalmologist who adjusts the refraction of light waves so that they retain their focal point on the patient's retina. The orthopedist who removes an arthritis-corroded hip and replaces it with titanium likewise encounters no philosophical concern. But in my daily practice as an oncologist, exploring the frontier between life and death, the gap between the organic and the inorganic is vast and insurmountable. It is, for most, the Abyss.

A patient I'll call Phillip illustrates how painful it is to live the last of life without a spiritual bridge—for him and his family, and for me—so to die on the far side of faith.

I met Phillip six years on in my career, before the epiphany I would later experience. He had worked for thirty years in Seattle, Washington as a computer analyst—a demanding career that had led to the collapse of his first marriage. When asked about his first wife he simply smiled and said, "We'd been married too long."

With his second marriage, Phillip wound down his career. He retired at age fifty-eight to pursue his lifelong dream of building a home in the woods beside a large green meadow and a meandering stream. For two years he lived the dream; he was only sixty when he came to see me, still robust and active, enjoying his new life in the country…and completely unprepared for the news I had to give him.

I diagnosed Phillip with a particularly aggressive case of non-Hodgkin's lymphoma. Aggressive and advanced: his kidneys were already failing. Without treatment, life would be short for this otherwise fulfilled and vital man.

Of course Phillip was not ready to give up. I assured him that with aggressive treatment I could give him more time. We began kidney dialysis and chemotherapy the very next day.

A Valiant Fight

Phillip fought courageously. Three days a week his nephrologist cleaned the urea out of his bloodstream with a super-filter blood dialyzer. I was

Phillip's other "medical mechanic," eradicating cancer cells from his bone marrow and lymph nodes with my chemotherapy.

Our hard work paid off. Four months along, we achieved a complete remission. He remained cancer-free for another ten months.

Then his cancer grew back. So we treated him again…and again… until finally Phillip's diseased cells resisted even the harshest chemotherapy in my arsenal. As the cancer began choking off his organs from the inside out, his strength deserted him. It became clear he and I could not win this battle. The time came when there was nothing left to do but infuse the morphine and wait.

By then I had been Phillip's doctor for eighteen months. I'd become very close to both him and his wife. We shared a delight in philosophical musings, and for fun would quiz each other on arcane etymology, Shakespearean quotes and world history.

I realize in retrospect that we were mainly just distracting ourselves from confronting the harsh reality of his condition. I acknowledge that in that process, and within the roles appointed to us, we became friends. So as I watched helplessly as Phillip's end drew near, I became all too painfully aware of the limitations of my skills as a practitioner of medical science.

Phillip no longer wanted to discuss etymology, philosophy or history. He no longer wanted to banter the pros and cons of the technology revolution he himself had helped to create. Phillip *just wanted to live*. He wanted to go back to his cabin in the woods with his beloved wife at his side.

But that was not going to happen. And where did that leave him?

Like me, Phillip had long before abandoned religious faith in favor of modern science. Unlike faith, however, science provides no refuge when hope is gone. Now he faced death with no prospect of Heaven, nor fear of Hell…no God, no angels, no spirit world, no source of final comfort. Phillip was utterly isolated.

So was I. His healer and confidant, I too was trapped in the secular world, imprisoned by definitions we shared—a worldview that left me with nothing helpful to offer him in this most desperate time.

Although Phillip was loved, he was still lost, soon to be banished to the waste heap that awaits all run-down *machines.* Failing machine and helpless mechanic, we each waited, along with his wife and family….

Phillip's twenty-one-year-old daughter made frequent visits to the hospital to be with her father, determined to stay close by until the end. A dance instructor, she talked at length about her father's condition and what it meant to her. As I was sitting with her at Phillip's bedside, watching him die, I vividly remembered a favorite Jackson Browne song, "For a Dancer." In that moment, every word of a special verse rang true…Browne's woeful melody laments the excruciating uncertainty of the dying in the modern age of existentialism, and this very uncertainty was gripping at Phillip's throat (and mine) as he moved oh so slowly and inexorably down the slippery slope of his physical demise.

Even worse for me was the song's reminder of the penetrating sense of stupidity and helplessness that engulfs the caregivers of the doomed, who finally have to acknowledge the ultimate failure of their efforts to rescue their loved one. *My failure* in particular: once I had been so proud of my intelligence, of the great effort expended to memorize the 50,000 odd facts I'd learned to become an oncologist. Now cancer revealed how shallow my "vast" knowledge was, how insignificant my skills and expertise. In comparison to my great foe, I was just plain stupid…

I listened to Browne's song that night on my way home from the hospital, and for many nights after that, often crying alone in my car.

I wept for Phillip, and for his wife and daughter. And I wept for myself, I'm afraid, because at the peak of my powers professionally, I could not save him, as I could not save Leslie, and oh-so-many others like them.

Science wasn't everything. And it wasn't *enough.* I understood that. The stark, sad emptiness of Phillip's spiritually-deprived death pounded into me the fundamental inadequacy of my analytic scientific knowledge and the medical model's *mechanistic* description of life. I was consumed by the same conflict I had faced with Leslie, the dilemma that had prompted me to leave behind a promising career at the great university in order to find answers to questions I could barely articulate, except to again say to myself, "something is missing, I am sure of it!" It was as if Phillip's cancer had whispered to me—*something lies hidden*—and I could not escape the certainty of that feeling. If I had no clue what that *something* might be, I knew it was important—an elemental part of dying that I could sense, but not yet apprehend. And that feeling of ignorance—the conviction that I failed to see and understand—haunted me through my despair and frustration and grief. It sounded an echo to words I heard too clearly in my mind: I failed to save.

Little did I know at the time, but hearing that whisper and echo was a crucial first step.

Faith, Reborn

Over the years I have attended to so many patients like Phillip. Each time at the end, I ached and cried with and for them and their loved ones. Every case made me more aware of the limitations of modern medical science.

But with each case *something* within my heart was slowly coming back to life. The beauty of childhood innocence, a wonder at life's mysteries, visions from a time of naïve faith…long abandoned by my intellect…began to stir again within me. At times they seemed to create just a faint resonance to the emotions that come to a doctor late at night, in the half-lit room of the dying, as he consoles a grieving widow-to-be, powerless to change the inexorable decline of her loved one. Other times, they moved me with spring tides of yearning, a ferocious need to divine an answer to the mystery of cancer.

Whatever it was, that answer lay beyond the realm of science, because science had none to offer.

I accepted that, in time. But I also knew this: unlike my colleagues, I could not continue trying to find solace in the next great offering from the pharmaceutical industry. That expectation—and the way it influenced my relations with patients—had troubled me at MD Anderson from the day I had dutifully conveyed to Leslie an optimism I had reason to doubt. But now I was no longer an initiate compelled by convention and the presumed wisdom of those more experienced. Phillip and a thousand other patients had taught me an imperative: Cancer is a terrible foe, but it is *not* the true enemy….

Something lies hidden. But…what?

I would learn. I will describe how that happened in happier stories. But I will introduce the idea here: *The real enemy is the fear of death, a fear that can only be overcome by recognition that we each have a soul that will never die.*

This is the ageless teaching of all the great religions. But in our modern world of science, medicine and technology, the purity and simplicity of that ancient message has been drowned out, and, for many, including Phillip and me, entirely lost. I abandoned that great truth in favor of the power of science and modern medicine. This book is of course the story of my journey back to the recognition of my spiritual birthright. My hope is that it will awaken others lost the same way.

This isn't an easy journey. It certainly wasn't for me; and as my friend died I could not yet imagine the power and wonder of my ultimate realization.

Tragedy initiated this quest. More tragedy drove me onward. That is, of course, a kind of flight; but at last "angels" guided me toward a glorious conclusion. At least I refer to them as "angels." In an earthly sense they were...

Patients. Ordinary people—trust me, you don't know any of their names. Angels *to me*...whose lessons I promised to pass on.

I wandered far afield for a time, searching for the source of whispers and echoes. A journey of a thousand steps....

Early on I avoided the more traditional spiritual resources I'd left behind. I still was cynical and not ready for them. By luck, or (you guessed it) by Providence, one of my closest friends at the time, a surgeon with whom I worked, urged me to take a chance and read Carlos Castaneda, that iconoclastic icon of the 60's movement.

Castaneda's stories describe his own improbable transformation as he pits his guile as a modern scientist against the sorcery of of an old Indian medicine man, Don Juan Matus. In Castaneda's masterpiece, *Tales of Power,* Don Juan taunts Castaneda for his stubborn loyalty to the strictures imposed by contemporary empiricism, insisting that his student's lifelong indoctrination in western science has left Castanada unable to "deviate from the path they've lined up for you...your thoughts and your actions are fixed forever in their terms. That is slavery." Eventually, Castaneda learns from Matus that there is another path—to "freedom." So enlightened, Castaneda himself would spend years traveling and writing about his own long journey toward "a separate reality."

Castaneda's words to Don Juan struck me profoundly: he was right. Doctors and their patients have both become captives of "scientific materialism," the modern-day dogma that denies the existence of anything spiritual or mystical, and in particular, the existence of *the soul*.

Castaneda's insight helped me see beyond confines "fixed forever in their terms." His encouragement opened my mind to the *possibility* of discovering that vital missing element in contemporary cancer care, along with the possibility that by sticking to a "rigid path," I had lost direction. Now my goal was clear, even if my course was not: to find my way to a more inclusive model for understanding life itself. Only then could I finally make sense of cancer…for me, and especially for my patients, that they need not succumb to fear and futility on their deathbeds. For what more could I hope?

It was and is as the renowned contemporary author Wendell Berry writes in *Life Is a Miracle*:

> For the human need is not just to know, but to cherish and protect the things that are known, and to know the things that can be known only by cherishing.

As a cancer patient, survivor, or surviving loved one, you've already been challenged mightily. You've been through so much, yet there is still a long way for us to go together. Through the stories of Phillip and Leslie, you've already taken big steps. Only one more sad tale to go; if you can keep your heart and mind open, I'll promise to bring to you a new understanding that may banish your fears, even in the face of death.

It's all about listening to whispers and echoes, which is how I myself first learned of… *The Undying Soul*.

Chapter Five

⌒

BENJAMIN: WHY OH WHY?

BENJAMIN SAT IN AN EXAM ROOM waiting for a status report from me on his quarterly cancer check-up. I sat at my desk in my office just down the corridor, reviewing his chart–the newest X-ray and test results. His old tumors were back. Ben had no idea. I had to go and tell him.

What's always the most difficult part of my job was harder still with Benjamin. We'd been through so much together during the three-and-a-half years since he was first diagnosed. Even back then, his condition was quite serious. Benjamin was far younger than the average colon cancer patient. Most patients get the disease in their late sixties or older. Benjamin had been forty-four, with a wife and two teenage daughters.

When the gastroenterologist found Benjamin's tumor, he referred Ben to a surgeon who removed it with an uncomplicated operation. Unfortunately the cancer had already spread to the lymph nodes in Benjamin's abdomen. Under the microscope, these cells looked angry— grossly misshapen, dividing rapidly, ready to spread into his body and cause widespread harm.

I told Benjamin I wanted to attack his cancer with my chemo drugs. He had a demanding job; he wanted to go to his daughter's soccer games across the state. So initially Ben resisted treatment: "God damn it, I don't have time for this, Dr. Iacoboni!" he told me emphatically. I told *him* that if what he wanted was time, he'd better take my advice. It was going to be chemotherapy…or death.

Benjamin took the chemo, the full six months I prescribed. He made it through without any major complications. After that it was smooth sailing…for a while. But I knew his prognosis was iffy, so I kept a close watch.

My vigilance paid off. Nine months later a follow-up CAT scan detected two new spots in his liver. If we hadn't detected these so early, Ben would have died within months. Instead, the surgeon went back in and carved out all of the visible tumors.

I knew we'd dodged another bullet. And I knew there were more to come: this initial relapse meant Ben would certainly die from the cancer someday, because once a cancer relapses, it will do so again and again.

I tried to explain that to him, when he asked me about his prognosis after the second operation. But every time I broached the possibility of his eventual demise, Ben stopped me cold. It was a lot like talking to Leslie and Allen. Ben just wouldn't hear it: "Doc, don't say things like that. You know I have to keep on living. So you just do whatever it is you do to keep me going. I'm counting on you."

I didn't blame Ben for his denial. There he was in my office, a relatively young, tanned, well-muscled man, looking and feeling great, with an adoring family waiting for him at home. How could he imagine what lay in store?

He couldn't. "I'm going to beat this thing, Doc. Just wait and see."

Six months after the liver surgery, almost like clockwork, new cancer spots appeared—there in his liver and now also in his lungs. With such an "angry" cancer from the start, I wasn't surprised. This tumor type grows slowly in the elderly, and ushers them gently into the grave. But when rogue cells get going in a young, healthy host, the result is like a lightning strike on dry timber in August. The conflagration rages out of control until it consumes itself, taking the entire hot, dry forest with it.

Benjamin was that forest. I could put out the flames here and there, delaying the process for short periods. But then the wind would shift, and the fire would race up another draw, jumping the break hell-bent...

The certainty of failure doesn't mean we don't fight. To get an advantage I infused my special new chemo formula directly into Ben's liver. I also had the thoracic surgeon pluck the accessible tumors from Ben's lungs, and the radiation oncologist hit the rest as hard as he could with high-energy gamma rays. So again we beat it back, achieving another hard-fought remission. Again we celebrated. For moments at such an uplifting time I even began to think maybe Ben was right. Maybe we *could* win.

It's hard not to let people pump you up with their optimism, especially when that's accompanied by praise, I suppose. But it comes with a price. While Ben expected that I would always triumph...I knew that high hopes didn't change his odds.

So there we were, just three months after our latest victory, a total of three-and-one-half years since it all started...Ben waiting for word, me sitting at my desk with the evidence in front of me...his cancer was back...just as if we had left coals smoldering in the forest, waiting to flare up: Ben was on fire.

Again...but now things were different. I had given him all the chemo his body could tolerate. In fact, the last round of toxic treatments created complications that required weeks in the hospital to help him recover.

Ben knew that. But by now I knew Ben, and that he would still be optimistic. Thanks to this last hiatus, the man sitting down the hallway would be upbeat, expecting to make this checkup a quick visit. If I would just tell him all the tests were negative, we'd say goodbye till the next three-month appointment.

Could I blame him?

Of course not. It's human nature—and especially Ben's nature. But sadly, it's also the nature of *cancer*.

And that's a peculiarity that cancer doctors have to recognize. With any serious disease, the worst part about being a patient is the lack of control over so life-threatening a condition. But the slow, gradual nature of cancer's progression seems to give many folks the impression that they can somehow alter the process. No one gets this notion when a coronary artery suddenly clots or when a diverticulum bursts and starts bleeding profusely. Cataclysmic and abrupt, these medical events don't leave you with the same sense of having any opportunity to somehow *willfully* change the clinical course.

To be sure, diet, exercise, mood adjustment and an overall healthy lifestyle are important strategies to employ in the battle against cancer. Clearly, these methods can play a vital role in cancer *prevention*. But once a cancer is full-blown and out of control, as it was in Ben's case, the more drastic measures of surgery, radiation and chemotherapy become necessary.

Benjamin's strategy for exerting control over his cancer was positive thinking, even wildly positive. Despite his two relapses, he continued to manifest confidence and optimism. It made a certain kind of sense: Ben had defied death twice and survived.

That Ben intended to continue surviving was obvious when at last I trudged down to the exam room to discuss his current—terrible—test results. As always, Ben immediately attempted to assert control by starting off the conversation on his terms: "Let's see those scans, Doc. I'm feeling *so* good!"

Not so, a few minutes later. Ben was crushed. Not only were there new tumors in his liver and lungs, now the cancer had spread to his spinal column.

Ben could barely believe it. He'd been so intent on hearing good news that he'd scheduled time for just a brief visit and had come alone; we had only minutes to consider options—more chemo, more surgery, more radiation. Then he was out the door, staggering a little while talking on his cell phone, telling his wife what he'd just been told.

What were they going to do? He was too busy at work to take time off for treatments! The girls were getting ready for prom and graduation…

When it sank in, however—and it did—Benjamin's optimism was finally shattered.

It was all downhill from there. Benjamin's body was more weakened from previous treatments than he had let on to me—and probably to himself. Now, with cancer growing back all over his body, he was left with little energy to muster against this new attack.

Our only option was to resume the chemo, and at his request we did. I didn't believe it would do him much good, but a beaten Ben wasn't ready to surrender. His condition sputtered at first, and then steadily spun out of control. He was in and out of the hospital, first with pneumonia, then a bleeding ulcer, then an inflamed pancreas. I knew we were nearly out of time for my poor Benjamin.

Yet each day that I saw him in the hospital he had that same quizzical look of disbelief in his eyes. His vast optimism turned into a special kind of denial, complete with questions: When was he going to get *better*? How come I couldn't fix things again? He simply *had* to get out of the hospital to take care of business and be with his family.

One day he broke down while I was in his room. We shared a long and sad commiseration. "Why, God, must I suffer with this?" he wondered aloud. Ben knew: he was dying, and I was powerless to help. So all I could do was sit at his bedside while he wept. And cursed. And wept some more.

As with Leslie, then Phil…I had no answers for him. I didn't know anyone who did.

Benjamin never left the hospital again. He died about a week later, delirious from fever, toxemia, and morphine. It was a gruesome, mournful sight. His wife stayed with him day and night. She said little to me, but I suspected that, unlike her husband, from the beginning she had known what he was up against.

I couldn't speak to Benjamin during his final days; he was incoherent. But I could see the anguish in his bewildered, terrified, and pleading eyes. I tried to reassure him with just my physical presence, but this didn't give him nearly the comfort he needed. He was spiraling away while I sat helplessly and watched, also inconsolable. As before with Phillip, I thought to myself that I felt helplessly overmatched against his disease.

Finally, Ben's suffering ended. At 2:00 a.m. a call came from his ICU nurse. "Dr. Iacoboni, your patient Benjamin 'Jones' has just passed away."

How I wish I'd known then what I know now. Had I, it might well have all gone quite differently.

Cast Out of Paradise

As hard as it was to lose Ben in that way, after those three-plus years we'd been together, the drama and intensity of that experience just strengthened my resolve to keep searching for the discovery I was yet to find—a discovery that might provide the kind of answers that might prevent patients like Ben, Phillip, Leslie and so many others like them from dying in that awful way. It wasn't so much the fact of their deaths that bothered me. Rather, it was the fact that they died without the comfort of finding peace within their hearts and souls before they passed on. After Ben I vowed to myself that I would find a way to comfort the dying and not fail them. I embraced an unswerving commitment to show them the reason for our lives beyond the materialists' narrow, spiritually crippling worldview. But *what was it* that we were all some-how missing, and *where* would I find it?

The cancer experience is so incongruous with our modern lives. In our busy, productive, high-tech-powered pursuits, we don't seem to need a God, any God, for anything…until we get cancer. Cancer sends us hurtling back to the Middle Ages, where we are at the mercy of the elements. Then all of a sudden we *do* need God. The problem is that we've lost track of faith in the hustle and bustle. This simple and hum-bling truth kept haunting me. Finding our way back to faith was clearly what was needed, but how to do so was exactly the great mystery, the unanswered question. Somehow, I had to get on the path to that holy destination, and *discover* whatever there might be out there that could bring peace to my patients, and to myself.

Sadly, "somehow" doesn't provide solace or guidance: I still seemed to be wandering in circles in the wilderness. I needed a guide to show me the way, because I was just too stubborn and blind to find out the truth of *The Undying Soul* by myself.

For years I wondered who that might be, where and when I might find him or her. Sometimes I just couldn't tell if I would ever find my way. I had no idea what would finally happen to my search.

Then I met Pavel.

Chapter Six

~

PAVEL:
THE GUIDING LIGHT

A SIMPLE FARMER NAMED PAVEL TISHKOON arrived from almost 10,000 miles away—literally the other side of the planet. In the most improbable of encounters, this gentle man came into my life as a cancer patient, only to serve as my first and most powerful spiritual guide. To me he was an angel, truly Heaven-sent. There can be no other accounting for our relationship and the profound way in which it changed my life forever. To put it plainly, he taught me that there was another way to die, and more importantly...*another way to live.*

Pavel came from the Ukraine, where he had lived in the shadow of the Chernobyl nuclear reactor. There he and his family had worked the land, caring for their livestock and tending their crops.

Then there was that terrible accident—Chernobyl's meltdown, the worst nuclear-power disaster in world history, from which escaped a cold dark cloud of radioactive precipitation that visited Pavel's countryside. Tomatoes turned yellow, green beans turned red, and his fields of wheat shriveled. All were radioactive, of course, yet Pavel's wife and the other women ground the polluted grains into flour for their daily bread. And they ate the oddly colored vegetables.

They had no choice. They ate what they grew, or starved.

Given that background, it's hardly surprising that Pavel developed a radiation-induced leukemia from the contaminated food. He wasn't alone or remarkable. Doctors at the poorly equipped, under-staffed and overwhelmed local hospital told him the obvious. They gave him pills with instructions to take them for a few weeks, then sent him home to die from a low-grade leukemia that would have been considered easily treatable in the United States. And Pavel would have done so, as did thousands of others during that era.

Pavel, however, found a different path to take. He was related to Russian immigrants who had settled in Walla Walla, Washington, where I then lived and practiced. Pavel's family members told their church about his condition, and that he would die without appropriate care. Church officials and town residents appealed to the State Department through their congressman, Tom Foley, then Speaker of the House. Speaker Foley secured compassionate dispensation and a passport for Pavel, who was flown to Walla Walla for treatment.

That's when I became involved. The church called my office, as did Pavel's family. They had no money to pay for medical services, but hoped I would see Pavel anyway. Realizing how many people had sacrificed time, effort, money and political favors to have this man brought to the United States, I was happy to play my part in the noble effort to help him. I understood this would require substantial time and resources. What I was not prepared for—what I could not imagine—was just how tremendously rewarding our interaction would become. Pavel was to teach me how to return to faith, and set me on the path toward my discovery of *The Undying Soul*.

Pavel arrived in our town and was immediately admitted to the hospital. I reviewed his most recent blood tests, alarmed to discover that three quarters of his red blood cells were depleted. The normal range for an hematocrit (red blood cell level) is 38-45: his was 10. Pavel had severe anemia. Given this great danger, I went to see him straightaway.

At my first meeting with Pavel, I encountered a wall-to-wall throng of Eastern European family members and friends. Many of the women wore dresses fashionable in the farming communities of their origin; the men sported unusual-looking, fur-lined hats. Everybody seemed attentive, somber and clearly excited to see the doctor arrive. It took me a minute to navigate through them and meet Pavel's gaze.

What I saw when our eyes first met was far from what I expected, especially given the conditions described in his medical chart. Despite Pavel's serious condition, I could see no obvious signs of illness or distress in him. His face was worn and weathered, but his expression looked open and happy. Pavel bore an expression as calm as that of the Pope's. And although I expected that he would be weak and feeble with such a low blood level, the moment he saw me he leapt out of bed.

I saw then that he was small in stature, about 5'2", dressed in baggy trousers and a tattered faded blue sweater that had seen better years. He grabbed my hand and shook it hard enough for me to feel the calluses on his palm. And then, slowly and ceremoniously, he bowed his head.

While I understood how he and his family might feel about his being given all this medical care that his own country had denied him, I found myself taken aback by such formal deference. I assured him by word—and then, discovering he spoke almost no English at all, by body language—that no bows were necessary.

Pavel smiled slightly, offering me an expression that spoke as clearly and as plainly as possible: this isn't about what's formal or necessary, it's about appreciation...

And, in a word, *grace*.

That's a remarkable message to convey with such a simple exchange. But it could not alter the news I'd brought to him: through an interpreter, I explained to Pavel that because his leukemia had been neglected so long it was too late to expect a cure. I was, however, optimistic that we might be able to control the disease, at least for a while.

Of course, that was a gentle way of reporting a certainty I soon realized Pavel understood: lack of treatment had left him at the end stages of what should have been a manageable disease. Now I could only buy him time before he died.

We started right away. The blood transfusions we gave him that day corrected Pavel's severe anemia. Even better, the first round of chemotherapy worked magic on Pavel's chronic lymphocytic leukemia. After several chemo cycles, he achieved a complete remission.

"Complete" is a deceptive word in cancer care. *Complete but temporary* is what to expect with cancers that have progressed to an advanced state before treatment begins. By that late stage these cancers have developed chemo-resistant clones out of the original cancerous cells. These "super-clones" grow, divide and become unresponsive to the therapy, creating a hopeless situation.

In the words of *any* language, "it was only a matter of time."

A Marvelous Gift

Three months after I met Pavel, during the remission phase when he was feeling well, he invited my wife and me to dinner in the home where he was staying. We accepted, presuming we could manage the language barrier one way or another. And with the help of Pavel's bilingual relatives, translation was not a problem.

As Pavel explained it, with help: before leaving the Ukraine for America, he realized it was unlikely he would live long enough to compensate his caregiver. This troubled him, so he asked an artist friend to hand-carve a unique thank-you gift.

That night after dinner, Pavel presented this gift to me: an elegant wooden eagle, sculpted in his native lindenwood.

It stands in my study today, three feet tall, with a wingspan of four feet. (Because of its size, Pavel had to separate the wings from the body in order to smuggle it in.) It's truly magnificent, and every day it reminds me of this man, and what he taught me.

But as much as I value that eagle, it was not his greatest gift.

Like almost all of my patients, Pavel was a Christian. I had known other Christians who had faced their deaths fearlessly, but only a handful. Unfortunately, the majority of patients I'd watched die from cancer did not seem to derive significant comfort from their faith at the end...

Until my experience with Pavel. Unlike others, his faith served him astonishingly well. He faced death without anxiety and, even more amazing, seemingly with eagerness and wonder.

Pavel's effect on me stemmed in part from his unfamiliar ethnicity and culture—that quality of the exotic. But I truly believe his personal qualities transcended that. Pavel was a simple man of extremely humble means, but his first and most lasting impression on me was of a phenomenal strength of spirit. Diminutive in size, with clean but shabby apparel, Pavel carried himself with strength and stature. His gaze was always calm and happy. His manner was always relaxed, gracious and deferential.

This appearance was hardly for show. Over time, cancer strips away all kinds of veneers; but through the entire duration of his prolonged treatments, Pavel never once complained. I could easily see how much he was suffering physically, but all he expressed was profuse, sincere gratitude.

Beyond all that, Pavel radiated a love of life that I have witnessed in very few people. Unable to speak to me in words, he communicated through the light in his eyes, his easy smile, and his contented attitude. He interacted with everyone this way, not just me.

He radiated a pure love with body language alone. Financially poor as I knew he was, he was in spirit one of the richest men I had ever known.

And how I wanted to understand that richness. Now in the middle of my career, I was searching for some kind of spiritual understanding, one that Pavel had obviously attained, as demonstrated in the way in which he faced his difficult life and his tragic illness. I desperately wanted to talk to Pavel about it. I was eager to learn his secret. I wanted him to share with me the source of his wisdom. But intimate conversation with Pavel was impossible. While members of the local Russian community could interpret medical matters, the conversations I had in mind could not be translated. I certainly couldn't probe his mind and soul through an intermediary.

Upbeat in the Face of Death

Just as I had anticipated, after nine months of treatment, the chemotherapy I employed against Pavel's leukemia began to lose its effectiveness. I could no longer control Pavel's cancer; and so…his death was steadily approaching. This filled me with regret. *But not Pavel.* All the while, he remained upbeat, happy and gracious.

I should note here that it's common in my practice for family members to report that patients appear far less robust at home than they seem during office visits. It's almost as if these patients hope that by showing off vigor, I will support them in their denial of death. Sometimes I offer them this confirmation. Sometimes I don't. It depends on how fully I am deceived, or how much I feel they need me to believe. Pavel was never like that. He was always gentle and sincere, and his optimism never felt forced in any way. When his dying body sagged, and his energy began to ebb, he didn't fight it. He just let it happen.

This struck me as profoundly like Zen—a worldview I was studying in depth at that time in my spiritual search, as an alternative to the traditional western religion I'd found so disappointing. Later in my search I would discover numerous similarities between Christian and Zen mysticism, and in retrospect come to realize that the universality of mysticism, East and West, was one more thing Pavel was teaching me. At that time, however, I imagined Pavel to be a kind of Zen master—an appealing and satisfying fantasy.

I'm sure that was partly because our inability to have actual conversation made him seem inscrutable—at least at one level. His expression came through those gestures that transcended the limitations of language. I have no idea how Pavel would have felt about my Zen fantasy: from his background, I guessed he had not the faintest notion of what Zen masters or believers in Zen principles think about or do. But then, I reasoned, even Zen masters say that *trying* to become a Master is impossible. It only comes naturally when one allows it to happen by itself. In other words, Pavel might have achieved that high plane of spiritual realization that characterizes a Zen master even though he never studied Zen.

While Pavel never feigned feeling better than he actually did, the signs of his deterioration were sometimes obscured by his inner strength. It was not bravado. Rather, his unique self-control and serenity made it more difficult for me to get a handle on his condition, especially since I was tempted toward denial in his case. But worsening lab reports told me the real story, so I was not fully misled even when his demeanor concealed the seriousness of his condition.

That real story looked awful. Suddenly, Pavel's spleen tripled in size—a clear-cut manifestation of the rapid cell growth; his leukemia was growing out of control. Within a month Pavel's spleen grew from the size of a potato, about normal, to that of a watermelon. In response I gave him stronger chemotherapy. That treatment was not *too* harsh— and patients do sometimes respond. But his illness was too far along. The chemo-resistant cancer cells relentlessly took over, and began to choke the life out of his body.

He was ready to die. And the process would not be easy.

Confronted with the certainty of a painful death like this, I want my patients hospitalized so that I can better control their miseries medicinally. Pavel accepted this recommendation and was admitted to the hospital for his last days. Perhaps this was easier for him, since he wasn't anywhere near his native country, so dying "at home" wasn't an option. But perhaps he agreed partly because he had come to trust me, and we both took comfort in each other's presence. I know that's how I felt—that our bond was so strong we would be glad to be together at his end.

When disease progresses to this stage a sort of dread spills out from the patient's room, flowing like lava down the hallways. You can sense the whimpering and teeth gnashing before you enter the patient's room. It is easier, I'm sorry to admit, to stay away when you can, avoiding sorrowful family members by making rounds late at night, often when the patient is asleep. I can slip in and touch a forehead, jot a note, chat with the nurse, and leave without becoming mired in the misery of the situation.

I had anticipated that this time it might be different with Pavel, so I went to see him right after supper, though I knew that was in the midst of visiting hours. Indeed, as I approached Pavel's room I found family members standing in rows in the hallway, the women swathed in their Eastern European shawls, flowing dresses and scarves. It was much like our first meeting, a sort of a cultural spectacle, now charged with approaching drama.

Like that first time I met Pavel, I had to work my way through a crowd to the bed. Everyone surrounding him had bowed their heads, so I did the same, staring mostly at the floor as I strode forward. When at last I shuffled through, I raised my eyes and looked directly up at Pavel's.

What I saw was almost miraculous. This *dying* man was sitting up in bed, his hands outstretched, beaming at all those gathered. He was happy, smiling and nodding, comforting all the sad people around him. His body ruined, eaten out from within…still he projected complete and utter spiritual contentment, despite the fact that physically he was dying. And while I could not understand his words, it was clear he was reassuring his friends and family members that everything was…fine.

For a time I could only stare in awe. At last I returned his broad smile and grasped the warm hand he held out to me. And then, again—as he had done at that first meeting—Pavel bowed his head, in a gesture I knew was meant to express to me his gratitude for everything I had done for him throughout the eight months we'd known each other.

Usually I feel frustrated and gloomy when all that I have provided through medical science proves inadequate. Certainly that's how I felt with Leslie, Philip, Benjamin and countless others. Not this time. As you'll soon see, this time "death" was completely different from what it had ever been before in a thousand previous episodes.

I could say nothing, and anyway Pavel wouldn't understand my *words*. He still held my hand when he raised his head. Then he did something he had never done before: he looked up at me and raised his eyebrows, not in complaint, but by way of extending affirmation. That's what I saw and felt. No interpreter intervened, so he spoke through his brightly gleaming eyes. His message was subtle but indisputable: that everything was…wonderful.

In that moment, I felt as though I could reach out and touch Pavel's soul, because that night his spirit was more tangible than anything else in the room. And there it was, perfect in that moment—the lesson I'd looked for. It was as if he had handed his heart to me. I sensed it beating in perfect rhythm, swelling the room with joy and exhilaration.

Suddenly I realized what Pavel had come to teach me: belief in the soul was *absolutely the only* way to make sense out of this situation. That was what I wanted and needed to learn from Pavel—his secret.

For years my intellectualism had prevented me from acknowledging the existence of the soul, and now all at once the "self-evident truth" of *The Undying Soul* was undeniably on display before my very eyes.

I never left his side. I stood in silent rapture at his bedside for half the night, feeling absolutely no sense of sadness or despair, like I had felt on so many countless nights in the past with the dying.

During that vigil I observed for the very first time in my career the rare and overwhelming beauty of a spiritually contented death. Pavel's very soul in death was made clearly manifest to me, as real as it had been for him throughout his life. It was at the moment of his passing that I first realized that it is during the slow death of a cancer patient when a humble observer can witness so miraculous a revelation as the undying soul's ascension.

In this unique type of slow death, the type of which I'd never seen before in fifteen years as an oncologist, the cancer patient allows him or herself to die naturally, without any of the sedatives that rob the consciousness of the "dying experience." I was able to stay emotionally and spiritually connected to Pavel during those three or four hours when he passed from this world to the next. And all that was required was to fix my gaze upon his, and watch the candlelight in his eyes slowly dim until that light was finally extinguished.

This was more mesmerizing to me than ten thousand ocean sunsets whereupon light fades to black. For decades in training and practice I had watched people die, thousands by now, each time wondering what they thought and felt. But in every case, they were rendered semicomatose by painkillers. Their eyes were shut to me, and little could be learned about their inner world as they passed into eternity.

Not with Pavel. His eyes were open.

And what I saw for the first time was this: somewhere along the way that night, as I stared intently into Pavel's eyes, and he so graciously and generously stared back into mine, it was as if he were intending to bestow a gift upon me with an impending revelation. Slowly the look in his eyes changed. His gaze became, to me, "unworldly," a look serene and selfless in a way that I'd never seen before in the eyes of another.

This wasn't the look of death, that chilling stare I'd learn to recognize during many years of medical practice. At first I thought he was becoming comatose, but when I checked his pulse it was still strong, and his breathing remained unlabored…nothing physical had changed for him. But soon his "unworldly" expression altered minutely, just enough to startle me with a wholly unexpected conviction…that I was watched by another sentient entity, someone *other* than Pavel the man—his ego or his persona. But who…or what…could it be?

Pavel no longer responded to my voice or my touch. But still his eyes shone into mine with a purpose that gripped me to the core. I became spellbound. What *could* it be? What *was* I witnessing? I held my breath as I hesitated to whisper to myself a truth that seemed self-evident…

I don't know how long it took me before I relaxed and with all my courage admitted it. *What was* I seeing in his eyes just before he took his last breath? Nothing physical, to be sure: I saw no halo, or angel's wings or lightning flashes; I heard no trumpets sound or music of the spheres. But I was so sure of it in that moment that I knew, and said to myself, and to Pavel, "Yes my friend, I see…'it'…

"…I see your soul."

In that moment of epiphany, of recognition and actualization … Pavel let go. His eyes closed, his breathing stopped, and the room fell still.

And yet still echoing, somehow.

What I learned this night absolutely answered that question that haunted me after the deaths of patients I've already described. Never again would I wonder if there was something more.

On this night of rapture what I saw was something I had long suspected but could never before observe. In a death such as Pavel's, the material corpus gradually fades as the spirit simultaneously makes its slow transition out of its earthly confines. No agony or sudden violence, no veil of coma or muting sedation obscures the process. Death at a snail's pace thus provides the unique opportunity to observe a "celestial" apparition. I say that *The Undying Soul,* long concealed, in death is finally made perceivable by one who has spent half a lifetime at the bedside of the dying—that this manifestation reveals a vital essence that has so long been missing in an era of science.

I remained in Pavel's dark room for another hour after his passing—mystified, captivated and speechless. I had been there. I had seen it—the perfect death—as Pavel left us to join his Creator. This small man in shabby clothes who had to eat radioactive food—what a wealth of spirit lived inside him. He had vanquished pain and sadness with his childlike heart and supernatural soul. What I had seen in Pavel's death by cancer was that the undying soul had at last been revealed.

Fear was inconceivable to this man. The conquest of fear in him was complete. And what was possible for him must also be possible for the rest of us. To this day, the impact of beholding Pavel's serenity in the process of his death has not left me. The experience surpassed such earthly ethereal spectacles as the most beautiful rainbow, sunset or perfectly formed ocean wave. It is difficult to accurately describe the wholeness of that revelation, but the angel in this man spoke to me, and let me know that life and death are one. He taught me that death can be simple, easy and happy. And he did so in a way that I had never before thought possible, for in his death he revealed to me the reality of his very soul.

Now I knew what I had to do. From that night forth I would search the eyes of the dying, hoping to find a way to help them experience that same pure, good passage from life to death that Pavel had demonstrated.

I would do everything in my power to make them aware, as Pavel had made *me* aware, of the reality of *The Undying Soul.*

The author with Pavel Tishkoon and grandson, circa 1995

Chapter Seven

⤳

PATRICIA

Staggered by the powerful impact of Pavel's serene death, I found myself poised on the brink of faith, certain that I had witnessed a spectacular event of incalculable dimension: an accepting soul that had achieved the sweetest release...

Still...I just could not...yet...take the leap to accepting faith. Even though I was buoyed by the conviction Pavel had given to me—a priceless gift—my arrogant intellect began a fierce campaign to inhibit my awakening, desperate to deny the existence—the very idea—of *The Undying Soul.*

Call it hubris, but I wasn't ready to discard my devotion to my undergraduate and medical school mentors, who frequently argued against any belief in a mystical entity like the soul. My rigorous dedication to science had itself become a kind of dogma, absolutely vital to who I believed myself to be—and seemingly a fundamental requirement for what I had become, *a doctor...*

Old commitments, habit—and my ego, I'm afraid to say—all kept me from yielding to the truth Pavel had so superbly and selflessly displayed. I waged arguments with myself, imposed impossible challeges, hypothesized explanations for what I witnessed watching him die...it just went on and on. I fixated on his foreignness: his language, demeanor and dress. All these made it easier to put his spiritual strength in a more extraordinary, less accessible context. Yes, he was plain and simple, dressed in a faded blue sweater, with holes in his shoes; he carved wood, grew wheat and tomatoes, all ordinary characteristics. But he came to me from the other side of the planet, and he never spoke to me in *words* I could understand, however I took his meaning. So, had it all been just a dream? Or perhaps just the imagination of an overworked, sleep-deprived doctor, desperate for some relief, something to sooth the daily drama of his patients' angst?

Because Pavel was so exotic I found myself comparing him to the Dalai Lama or Pope Paul II, comparisons certainly bordering on idealization. And even if these were fitting, I reasoned, what did it mean? How could I expect to ever ascend to that level of faith and spiritual wholeness?

Tough, confusing questions. Looking back, it strikes me how raw I was when Pavel came into my life, how unready, how much ground I had to cover in my search for faith, and those answers that I had left MD Anderson to find ten years before. Pavel's magnificent death pointed me squarely in that direction and motivated me to keep on searching, amplifying the questions I'd set out to answer earlier in my oncology career. Science—my science—could describe these painful, seemingly empty deaths; but science could not pretend to *give them meaning*.

Pavel had...for the first time in my career...given death a new meaning. Whatever my doubts, that much I knew at some level beyond reason. However vigorously my rational side attempted to thwart my acceptance of his mystical demonstration, over time my heart, mind and *soul* did slowly begin to yield. Pavel's gift gave me hope that my quest would someday lead to fruition, and that further guidance would arrive just as he did, to continue to lead me down the as-yet invisible path of the undying soul.

That's why I pasted a picture of the two of us onto the bookshelf in my office (see page 51). Whenever my work became overwhelming, that photo and his memory soothed my spirit and reminded me to stick with my quest. Pavel's ministry motivated me to rigorously re-examine my long-held atheistic stance.

I had attended college and med school at the dawn of "the biological revolution" in modern science, which preached that God was dead. Could it be I had been misled by my professors? Because of Pavel I revisited their dogma to study it anew in the light of my experiences and knowledge as a cancer doctor. And finally I was able to challenge myself with this fundamental question, "Could it be that we each really do have a soul, a spirit, one we can actually experience?"

In fact, my research during this time caused me to become far more sympathetic to the intellectual argument in favor of faith. But faith is certainly beyond the intellectual and the merely rational. Faith is the unity of spirit with conscious experience. For five years after Pavel's death, my subconscious kept trying to tell me, "Faith is real! The soul is real. You saw it! Pavel showed you. Wake up and admit it!" But would I listen?

Perhaps. Perhaps Pavel's ever-resounding message was slowly getting through. But I still couldn't seem to take the next step on my own. I tried to keep these disruptive, newly emerging emotions buried. But the once-strangling grip of my rational ego was steadily beginning to loosen. Still, I needed another angel to take me by the hand and show me the rest of the way. Without consciously realizing it, I was getting myself ready for my next spiritual mentor. On a subliminal level, I knew that something, or someone, was coming for me.

She was. Her name was Patricia.

The Diagnosis

"I'm very sorry to have to tell you this, Patricia. But unfortunately, you have a life- threatening disease called multiple myeloma."

When we met, her disease was at an advanced stage and already attacking her bones. It had already caused a fracture of her upper left arm bone, the humerus. Yet instead of crying or falling apart at the tragic news, Patricia assured me that I had nothing to apologize for. Then she thanked me for making the difficult diagnosis that had eluded her other physicians. At my recommendation, she immediately began a treatment program of chemo, radiation, and orthopedic surgery.

From that beginning I had an inkling that Patricia was special. But I was tempted to credit her substantial courage to the kind of denial new patients often exhibit at the early stage when they believe that your seemingly limitless medical powers can save them. Later, when you run out of chemo recipes as the cancer advances, fear usually breaks through.

Patricia and I did have our early successes. Her myeloma went into a brief remission. But the advanced stage of the disease and her physical frailty combined to make the effects of the chemotherapy especially harsh on her. Over the next few months she was in and out of the hospital with pneumonia, anemia and fever. All the while I wondered if it was really worth it. Even the best possible "success" could only buy her a very difficult year and then still end in death, at a cost of over fifty thousand dollars in medical care.

Through it all, Patricia never seemed worried.

Patricia was a quilter. Her devoted husband Karl was a beekeeper. They lived in a cabin on a small lot in a tiny town in the north woods. Her daughter, son-in-law and grandchildren lived in another small cabin on the same piece of ground.

Despite her frail bearing and simple lifestyle, Patricia and those who loved her were wealthy in the most important of ways. She had not lost her faith. She had no anxiety over her situation. She was always gracious and generous of spirit, despite enormous tribulation. Eventually, I had to admit that the courage she demonstrated when we first met was enduring, even inspiring.

Karl was always at her side. I knew I'd have to prepare him for Patricia's inevitable passing. But he too was not swayed. The two of them would sit together there in the chemo treatment suite, sewing, reading, humming and praying, never appearing concerned for themselves, always deferential toward their busy doctor.

Intrigued, I questioned them about their selfless serene attitude. In long discussions, I came to realize that their faith was real and sustaining. Patricia, so "meek and mild," just kept looking at me, apparently pleased to be under my care, almost contented, even while enduring a prolonged and indescribably painful death.

In a word, Patricia seemed *saintly*...and I eventually found myself besotted, and mysteriously inspired. In the days, weeks and months before her death, I couldn't stay away from her for long. I spent hours at her bedside, talking; and yes...at last...I was praying.

I had been raised as a devout Catholic, the grandson of Italian immigrants. Their children, my parents, taught me about faith, and how to pray. I stopped praying and believing in my early adult years. Beyond that, over time I'd come to mock prayer and religion.

Now after three decades wandering in the wilderness, I had been rescued—first by Pavel, and now by Patricia.

A Farewell Visit

The time came when I knew the end was near. So did Patricia and Karl. She wanted to die at home, so they stopped by my office to pick up supplies and medications for her final days, and to say good-bye. As always, they invited me to visit them, an invitation I always declined.

But not this time. I couldn't help myself. The formal office-farewell wasn't enough. I knew I had to see Patricia one more time; I said yes,

I would visit. And so it happened that I went to see her and Karl, on what would be the last Saturday of her life.

I took directions and checked maps. Patricia and Karl lived in tiny Hope, Idaho a town that occupied a saddle of a narrow mountain pass, on a lonely road that served as the only paved access into that remote part of the Gem State. A long drive, but as it turned out, so well worth it.

The fall air was crisp and delicate, suffused by the subtle fragrance of fallen leaves and moist earth. To this, add enchanting vistas of rivulets, beaver-dammed creeks and translucent blue-green ponds surrounded by seas of emerald marshlands. In the distance rose alpine peaks so high and jagged they looked surreal. As I drove I experienced the sense that I was entering a fairy tale, or even that I had stumbled onto the lost path to Eden.

Suddenly, rounding a wooded bend, a spectacular vista exploded into view—the massive expanse of Lake Pend Oreille, shimmering deep blue turquoise under the sun.

Stunning. Awe-inspiring. All it needed was a sound track to match the sweep of horizon; so, by force of habit, I switched on the music I'd brought to accompany this visit, Jackson Browne's song "For a Dancer." My anthem ever since Phillip and his daughter, those verses seemed to capture what I felt about the mystery and emptiness of dying.

"Dancer" began as I looked out at the lake. And in an instant I felt that fairy-tale quality, the marvelous feel of traveling a path to Eden and Patricia…*collide* with words of sadness and confusion, the crash of glory against despair…

My hand leaped out—I snapped "Dancer" off. This was not how I felt, nor how I would feel. This was…*wrong.*

I have never played that woeful song again.

I had grown. I'd found what I knew was missing in the drama that is cancer medicine. I knew that, unlike with Phillip, this meeting with

Patricia would not make me feel stupid and helpless when confronted by cancer.

I knew that I would never feel that way again.

Years before I'd wept alone in my car listening to Browne's song. Now, with beauty filling my eyes, I burst into tears again, overwhelmed this time with the joyful, emancipating realization that Patricia had delivered me forever from that empty, spiritless state of faithless, wistful wandering. And suddenly it felt like my once aimless and seemingly endless search was drawing to a rapid conclusion, quickly, mile by mile as I closed the distance to Patricia's home.

For so many years I had believed that achieving this state of exhilarating rapture was unattainable, and that those who made such claims were charlatans, simpletons or just delusional. But now, heading toward my beloved dying Patricia and what could have been a situation of overwhelming pain, I experienced what my literary hero Wendell Berry described as the greatest human need: "to know the things that can be known only by cherishing."

Instead of sadness, I felt euphoria.

In my usual state of analytical control, I would have struggled to explain to myself what was happening to me and why. But in those last twenty minutes of my drive to Patricia's home I transcended logic, analysis and deduction. I was overcome with a clarity of mind and spirit that had no need for these rudimentary methods of inquiry. Preparing to let go of a beloved patient *while my medical powers stood useless...*

I realized that spiritual clarity was Patricia's final gift, the miracle she had always intended to bestow upon me.

Patricia had erased in me all elements of doubt, fear and grief. In so doing she made it possible for me to accept and process the experience of her transcendent faith. And so, for the first time in my life, I realized that I was finally in control…of everything that mattered…despite being completely unable to control the course of disease in so dear a patient as Patricia.

I had not achieved this through the limited powers of science and logic on which I had relied my entire adult life. Instead, for the first time since I left behind my childhood beliefs, I had become an active participant in this limitless power of the spirit that Patricia had imparted to me. Far beyond any quaint metaphor, she was truly an angel Heaven-sent.

Still lost in my euphoria, I somehow was able to spot the painted wooden sign on the road that read, "Patricia's Quilts." I pulled off and parked on the dirt driveway. Back behind a row of half-grown junipers stood a trailer lit with dim yellow light. I walked up the rickety steps and knocked. Karl opened the door. His eyes beamed widely. "Patty," he said, "it's Doc. Dr. Iaconi is here. He's come to pay you a visit."

Patricia was in her bed. Her condition had deteriorated rapidly in the few days since her office visit. I had the keen sense that she'd held on just to see me once again. The house was dark and cramped. Her dutiful daughter sat silently at her bedside. I grasped Patricia's frail hand in mine, and gazed into her eyes, both of us finding it unnecessary to speak. I could tell instantly that she knew what had transpired during my journey to see her that day…

…And how she had changed my life forever. How she had made me aware of my own undying soul, which I had so foolishly abandoned through pride so long ago.

Eventually Patricia summoned enough strength to say, "I'm so glad you came!"

We sat there together for several hours, her daughter, son-in-law and Karl, as Patricia stared contentedly upward toward her Heaven, a splendor only someone of her saintliness could conjure in those thread-bare conditions. She was like Lao-Tsu, Jesus, Abraham, Buddha and Mahatma Gandhi, seeing beyond all things worldly. I simply sat in her presence, comprehending without thinking, knowing without questioning, appreciating without worrying, completely captivated in my "altered" state.

Finally it was time to go. After a final long look between us I got up, bent over to kiss her cheek, and left in rapture. That afternoon in that dark, crowded, humble place, I had felt my own Undying Soul, more alive and real than anything I had ever known before.

What Patricia told Karl

I had expected Patricia to live one or two more days at the most, and that is what happened. A few days after her death, Karl visited my office. "Doctor, I want you to know what Patricia said to me about a week before she died. She told me not to be mad at God for making her sick and letting her die." Choking back tears, he continued, "She said that the Lord gave her cancer so that she would meet Dr. Iacoboni and teach him about faith."

I was overwhelmed. I was speechless. Karl and I embraced in both commiseration and joy. Then we parted, both of us teary, trembling, and yet rejuvenated to the core.

Through Patricia, through Pavel and other inspiring children of God who have come under my care, I made the discovery that is the substance of this book. I "found" my own "lost" soul. I finally let go of my ego-driven pride. I no longer need it.

Now all I care about is helping others uncover and cherish their own resilient, undying souls. This is now the foundation of my medical ministry, and will remain so for the rest of my career as a cancer doctor...

From a Dream

As powerful and uplifting as was my experience with Patricia, I couldn't help feel a deep void in the weeks after her passing. I found myself moping my way through my daily rounds and bustling office practice. Of course, I was grieving her loss and so my reaction was pretty natural. I kept telling myself that I should have felt elated by the experience, but in such situations emotions are often irrational. I concentrated all my energy on processing everything she had taught me, and in so doing had little energy left over for my "day job." It finally got to the point where I had gotten quite exhausted, and found myself heading home early one evening, taking advantage of a rare lull in the intensity of my practice demands.

I went to bed and fell into a deep sleep. Toward dawn, I dreamed that I was at Patricia's gravesite, struggling to summarize in a prayerful homage all that she had meant to me. I slowly composed a poem in her honor, *and as it took shape, I became aware that I was dreaming.*

The power of my devotion to her memory forced me to "memorize" the poem so that I could capture it upon release from my slumber. I kept reciting it to myself over and over, hanging on to each verse as I ascended from my deep sleep through woozy drowsiness to a wistful wakening. I got up in the dark of predawn, drifted out to the study and scribbled down the words as I recollected them. Then, still sleepy and drained from the effort, I went back to bed and resumed sleeping, dreamlessly, until morning.

When I woke I wasn't even sure if all that had really happened. I went out to the study and there I did find the scribbled predawn writings that were still mostly dreamlike to me.

This poem to Patricia was the first I'd written in my entire adult life. I polished it up a bit in full consciousness, realizing all along that the light that shone in these verses was actually the light of Patricia's *Undying Soul,* which she so selflessly shared with me.

Poem for Patricia

She came in last fall a tremblin',
deep wrinkles made me sigh.
Then summer life was seeping,
this fall more sigh, then cry…

Redeemed by love's small favors
I lastly saw you smile.
You gave to us so freely
If only for a while…

Bluebonnets spray their wisdom
where mankind's wit is spent.
Your illness was so fleeting,
'till at last your body bent.

A broken body teeming
with love yet left to give.
We felt God's hand upon you.
He would not let you live.

I see the moonset glitters.
I know all beauty fades.
I wish I'd kept you longer
My own touched soul to save.

Now gone you've left us weeping.
My heart must pray for peace.
An angel once among us,
You've earned God's sweet release…

I pray you'll keep us warm here.
Once patient, now soul set free.
There will be those that follow,
who knows what more they'll need?

Bluebonnets whisper wisdom,
like that shone from your eyes.
Please keep me strong and faithful
'till ere I earn the prize.

Lone swan flies steadfast southward
'cross dampened cloudy skies.
Man's earthly labors limited
lest the harder that he tries…

I may yet see you sometime.
My Lord please keep me strong.
This tender pain-filled lifetime
can only last so long.

For once it seemed so distant
His heaven, 'ere this land.
You brought me so much closer
when first I took your hand.

Chapter Eight

 ⌒

CLARENCE:
NOTHING TO FEAR

AFTER PAVEL AND PATRICIA, I met Clarence. I will tell you his story by taking you into the heart of our doctor-patient relationship, the only way I can reveal something that I can't otherwise explain.

Nestled in the wooded hinterlands of frontier northern Idaho, the county hospital's Kootenai Cancer Center keeps three social workers constantly busy looking after the patients of six doctors, including mine. That's a high ratio of social workers to MDs, but their services are needed. I'll show you what I mean: "Clarence can't pay his electric bill. This is a request for a waiver on his electricity bill due to illness. Could you please sign this form for me, doctor?"

Margaret had a sweet smile but a forceful way of "requesting" my signed approval of all her aid applications. Tireless and dedicated, she was the best social worker I'd ever known. I tried to never miss an opportunity to learn anything about my patients that they confided in her. Confide they did; like I said, she had a sweet smile, disarming at times. She also doted on her clients…and they knew it.

I was surprised to hear that Clarence was broke. Through Margaret I learned that although he had a full-time janitorial job that provided health insurance, the pay was minimal. Also, when he divorced a few years before, he'd lost a good portion of whatever money he might have accumulated. Now he lived alone in a small apartment across town, where he soon might lose his electricity.

What was much more important to me than his finances, however, was that Clarence was a simple, friendly man, so self-effacing that I guessed he hadn't contested the divorce settlement…In a word, Clarence was *likeable*.

"Likeable" is what means the most to me as your doctor. The practice of oncology is fraught with all the emotional turmoil I've already described. And what can make it unbearable is when doctor and patient don't form the kind of camaraderie or bond of friendship that can get them through the unavoidable hard times ahead. Clarence arrived in my practice long after I'd lost interest in serving self-important patients. And I can tell you this: one of the best-kept secrets in medicine is the profound satisfaction one can find while doctoring the honest, self-sufficient populace of rural America.

Clarence himself filled me in on more details of his life and medical history. He'd spent two years in Alaska during the epic campaign to construct the great oil pipeline. One day while eating canned food in the work camp, Clarence got served the wrong lot of rations. That most feared of all poisonings, botulism, lay in wait. An hour after his meal, Clarence was nearly dead, gasping for air as the botulinum toxin began paralyzing his diaphragm. He survived, thanks mainly to the savvy camp M.D. who had seen this poison strike others in the crew. Clarence did make a full recovery and was able to resume work in the great North.

When I discussed this incident with Clarence it seemed like a remote footnote in his health history—a medical curiosity with no bearing on his current condition. Certainly it seemed less pertinent than this other aspect of his life: like a lot of men of his day, Clarence enjoyed his smokes. And he enjoyed them twenty or more times a day, for forty years, before they ever gave him a minute's trouble. Then all at once they did give him trouble…big trouble.

In fact, only twenty percent of smokers actually get lung cancer. The biggest health problems associated with cigarettes are emphysema and heart disease, which afflict almost all smokers if they don't quit before age forty. Like many, Clarence had a mild smoker's cough for a decade, so it took some time for him to notice that it seemed "different" lately. He had less wind, even for simple chores. Then he lost interest in food.

By the time Clarence saw a doctor for the telltale chest X-ray, he had dropped twenty pounds from his already-trim frame. Given his symptoms and habit, there was little doubt about it: Clarence had lung cancer. So he was sent to me.

The moment comes in every oncologist-patient relationship for the face-to-face "you've got cancer" talk. After thousands of these it's commonplace, I suppose, but never routine. I remind myself before each talk that this is the patient's first time hearing such news—and that having this conversation can be devastating.

I had that in mind with X-rays and lab test results in hand as I made the slow march down the clinic hallway to the exam room where Clarence was waiting. He stood and greeted me like an old friend. (As I said, it's a hidden secret how satisfying it is to doctor country folk.) I showed him the spot on the X-ray where his cancer was. I went through the lab tests. At last it came time to say what I came there to say.

"Clarence, I am very sorry to have to tell you this, but you have lung cancer."

For patients to show emotion upon hearing the news seems natural, even healthy. For doctors, showing minimum emotion is our standard procedure. As medical students and residents, we're taught to be good soldiers, trained to accept death with some detachment...quite literally as just another "biologic event." Doctors who can best manage this clinical circumstance are more likely to treat very sick people: cancer patients, for example. For oncologists, a certain reserve is required. So while bringing this sad news to Clarence I held my emotions in check, and watched for his reaction. Clarence was mildly upset. He was not, however, devastated. I guessed he had his suspicions; lifelong smokers often take a resigned approach, knowing their lifestyle probably caused the cancer. But you cannot presume. Sometimes patients don't immediately react, because they are stunned and speechless. Sometimes it's during later visits that their need for emotional support eventually emerges loud and clear.

That's okay too. Having cancer and facing the harsh treatment and the possibility of death can be terrifying. Accepting and understanding the diagnosis is an ongoing process that takes time.

With Clarence, I had another tough step to take during our initial visit. His cancer had advanced so far that it was now inoperable. So we had to make some immediate decisions about what treatment options besides the standard surgical approach might be best, an effort primarily aimed to keep him going for a year or eighteen months at best, but not likely much longer than that.

Clarence agreed to radiation and a not-too-aggressive trial of chemotherapy. We started without delay. For several months things went smoothly. As expected, he proved to be a low-maintenance patient. He was always pleasant, never needy, and constantly grateful. Eventually, I stopped expecting any delayed emotional outburst from him. In fact, I came to admire how this decent man of little means took the challenges of radiation and chemotherapy so easily in stride. That much I could see for myself, but for a while I didn't learn a lot more. Clarence lived by himself, and he always came solo to the office. For a time I even wondered if his lack of apparent worry stemmed from a feeling on his part that he didn't have much to live for. I imagined him alone in the world, scrubbing floors for a living, and not terribly interested in going on like that for another twenty years.

So *maybe* Clarence just didn't care…but for some reason that assessment didn't quite fit him. He was kind, considerate, and happy to be alive. I suspected there had to be more about him that I hadn't yet realized.

And indeed there was.

Clarence had been under my care for only six months when his condition took a serious downturn. That's not unexpected for his type and stage of cancer; we had never pushed too aggressively for a total remission. Still, I was disappointed when I had to tell Clarence that it was time to go to the hospital for several days of more specialized interventions.

He readily agreed. Fortunately, I was able to temporarily put the brakes on the growth of his cancer, but eight weeks after discharge I had to readmit him. Again we met with some success, but less this round. By then Clarence was bedbound…and it was clear to both of us that he was living on borrowed time.

By now I felt I knew Clarence pretty well. During our weekly encounters over an eight-month period we'd had plenty of time to bond. As a result, I was relaxed as I entered his hospital room for another "heart to heart." Clarence knew from the outset that I'd come to tell him he was dying. He could sense it, I was sure, yet I searched his eyes for fear and saw none. Nor was there resignation, remorse or depression.

Clarence was proving himself to be a man of profound emotional serenity, even in the complete absence of any outward religious leanings. I was deeply intrigued and wondered to myself, "Why is this?" As we sat through a brief silence, Clarence appeared to read my mind. "Y' know Doc, I'm just not scared. Do you want to know why?"

Boy, did I.

He smiled. "Remember when I told you about that time I got botulism?" I replied that certainly that was hard to forget, since it was a rare and spectacular medical event.

"You remember when I said that I nearly died before they revived me? Well what I didn't tell you then was this. When I was lying there, 'dead' I saw a bright light. It was the most beautiful light I'd ever seen. I felt myself pulled toward it. I wanted to touch it, and reached out for it. " He smiled again. "And that's when I came back to this world, and woke up in the hospital bed."

Clarence paused. "But I never forgot. Because I learned what it's like to die. I know. I've already done it and it's not bad at all. In fact, it was a beautiful, beautiful thing. That's why I'm not afraid. I've been to the other side, and I'm convinced that there's nothing to fear."

I sat there, incredulous. My first reaction was to wonder if he made this up, since it just sounded so much like what others have reported. But it didn't seem like deceit to me; nor did I get that impression when I sought and received his reassurance that what he was saying was true. In short, I found myself believing. Clarence wasn't a conniving man who would fabricate such a story. His description of the botulism poisoning was unassailable, for example. But more compelling by far...*Clarence had no fear.* He really didn't. Knowing death neared, he watched it approach without terror. Clarence wasn't a guru committed to finding a lofty spiritual plane, nor did he need to convince me of anything. Yet there he was, cool as a cucumber, explaining that he had been to the other side.

In Perspective: the Light Fantastic

Clarence is the only patient I've known who "saw the light" during a near-death episode. The common theme reported on this phenomenon is that it transforms the person involved, so that they spend the rest of their life free of the fear of death.

Like Clarence.

According to his biographers, Carl Gustav Jung, one of the greatest intellects of the twentieth century, had a similar experience. You might decide to doubt me and Clarence, but not the renowned C. G. Jung. Thanks to Clarence, I now had a first-person depiction of death I'd only read about, offered by somebody whose veracity I accepted…

I was overwhelmed that he'd trusted to me this insight into the true existence of *The Undying Soul.*

And I still think about it…every day.

Later I discovered that I was quite mistaken about Clarence when I wondered if he had anybody else to live for. About two weeks before he died I walked into his hospital room, and for the first time met his son, a shy and beautiful ten-year-old boy, at that moment tucked under his father's sheltering arm.

"This is my boy, Doc," said Clarence, gushing with pride.

I myself have three sons. I instantly understood that Clarence felt the same deep devotion to his boy that I feel toward mine. So he did have something very, very important to live for, and his courage was not due to some grim resignation resulting from an empty life. And for rest of his days, Clarence and his son were inseparable.

I found myself deeply moved while watching this loving son slowly lose his father. Clarence continually reassured him, and me. And the sentiments I witnessed and felt made me even more confident that Clarence's story was real, as was the great courage that his near-death experience inspired in him.

When I think about Clarence with his son, Pavel with his family, Patricia with her husband…I have to compare their experiences with those endured by Phillip, Benjamin, Leslie and the many other patients who seemed to die fearfully and spiritually deprived. Benjamin's reaction to the cancer diagnosis was extreme bewilderment. Phillip had been misled into denying his spiritual birthright. Neither was able to die with the peacefulness of Pavel, or in the process demonstrate Patricia's selfless love.

And what's even more disturbing is this: not only were Phillip and Benjamin real individuals and patients, they represent *most* of the patients whose deaths I've witnessed. And sadly, most of their doctors were like me, unable to answer the most fundamental question ever posed by mankind: "What is the meaning of my life, and my death?"

Clarence, Patricia and Pavel finally got through to me. They gave me their answer to the question I'd been trying to answer all those years since I left MD Anderson. And I think about them and their message constantly, as I attend to my patients through my daily hospital rounds and in the office. Most importantly, I think about the task they challenged me to accept.

The answer they gave was spiritual. Each affirmed faith and love, and the real presence of the undying soul. They utterly conquered fear, despair, and self-pity. They successfully penetrated my armor-plated atheistic shell, but not by way of my intellect. They got through by way of my heart, not my mind.

I truly believe with all humility that our meetings were not by chance. And I also realized that their generosity was not something I could accept without my offering something tremendously important in return.

Having quite literally given me back my faith, surely they deserved no small compensation. What, if anything, did I have in return to give to them that could be so valuable? What could I ever do to balance this debt? That would ever justify their trust and sacrifice?

Those questions have persisted in me, and driven me relentlessly for the past ten years. My most heartfelt wish has been to repay them all. But how?

In time, I realized what they wanted and needed from me, and what they were, by example, prompting me to do: "Go back, Dr. Iaconboni, and find the answers," I would hear them whisper. "Find the kind of answers only a scientist-turned-cancer-doctor can discover. Find out where modern science has gone off course and led mankind astray. Then put the pieces back together the way God meant them to be. Reunite faith, science, and medicine. Don't let your patients live in fear anymore. Liberate them to rediscover their undying souls.

"We have shown you the way, dear doctor. Don't let us down."

Chapter Nine

⁓

THAT SOMETHING MISSING

As a young doctor I indulged in the paradoxical activity of looking for spirituality in a world that I believed was godless. As a result, I found myself climbing mountains, hiking through forests, paddling down breathtaking river gorges and staring at brilliant ocean sunsets. The raw power, beauty and glory of nature can stir and inspire the dullest soul, as surely it did mine. My love of natural wonder began during my halcyon youth, the days of my childhood native faith. I had left that faith behind, but not my love of nature. To be sure, stars and seas and trees and alpine panoramas sustained me for many years. When you're between the age of eighteen and thirty-nine, your own internal exuberance needs little external affirmation. Yet a falling star, the haunting distant howl of a wolf, a pristine blue-white glacier or shimmering alpine rivulets…were always there to inspire awe, and to instill wonder and happiness when I most needed it. And need it I did, believe me, during those challenging times in my life when I otherwise spent endless hours at grueling hospital work, confined in that sterile setting, surrounded by the sick, the needy and the dying.

But as age and weariness naturally accumulate from the endless medical marathon that is an oncologist's life, the time must finally come when these restless spiritual wanderings require something far deeper than the occasional external glance at the wonders of nature.

I recall one such experience in vivid detail. I was standing alone on a ridge deep in the Colorado Rockies at 12,000 feet, looking out over the near-limitless expanse of the Continental Divide. This was the greatest physical grandeur I had ever seen. Jagged snow-capped peaks stretched endlessly toward the horizon, with not another person around for miles…

For years, spectacular vistas such as this one sustained me. It was enough, back then, to look out on nature's splendor and somehow know that despite all the suffering, pain and misery I attended to every day on the cancer ward, life was still good and beautiful. But this time what I experienced was different: a cold wind and hailstorm swept up across the ridge to assault me without warning. I had to hurriedly climb down from that precipice to safety, out of the paralyzing wind and blinding ice pellets.

As I huddled that night by my fire, alone at 10,000 feet within a protected escarpment, I realized that the natural world, raw in its beauty and power, remains detached and remote, cold and uncaring. I could stare out over those mountains for ten years and still feel isolated and alone. I could stare in wondrous awe at the panorama, yet still have to face my own existential impermanence, the realization of my own inevitable death. With that understanding I came to realize, as yet only in the vaguest way, that the mystery of life itself would not be solved by remaining separate from it. I wanted to internalize nature, to *become* those mountains. Yet when the coldness and harshness of that storm descended on me, I realized at last that my pantheistic quest for "oneness" was mere fantasy. For all of our nature and discovery shows and RV road trips, we all live indoors, by choice, venturing out only on rare occasions during clement weather.

Way back then I had no inkling that my frustrated spiritual wanderings would someday, finally, allow me to realize a fundamental truth enfolded in the mystery of cancer. Years later, as I pondered ceaselessly the wonder and magic of the deep faith that inspired Pavel and Patricia,

I kept asking myself: what made it different for them? They offered no overt revelations about the Gospel that had uniquely transformed them. In truth, there was nothing factually different in what they believed compared to all of my other patients, many of whom asked me to help them resolve the spiritual uncertainties which have emerged in this age of scientific atheism. "Where *is* God?" they so often asked.

So what was the difference? I had to know.

Meditating on this, my mind wandered back to those exuberant backpacking days of my youth, when I was always going after John Denver's "Rocky Mountain High, In Colorado." I recalled that day of the hailstorm, and the impasse that I had encountered while trying to find my spirit somewhere out there amidst the mountains, streams and forests. It occurred to me that my frustrations and spiritual emptiness were not unlike those my fearful patients experienced. Was there a connection? A parallel?

For several years the answer to this question remained obscure to me. It was only after my discoveries and research on the shortcomings of the scientific "proof" of atheism that the answer became self-illuminating.

And why not? It turns out that I was asking essentially the same question of both science and spirituality, but within entirely different frameworks, using languages that lacked common ground...which is why the self-evident truth lay hidden for so long. What I at last realized was that the essential ingredient that was missing in the worldview of scientific atheism was likewise missing in my secular "spiritual" pantheism quest. In both instances, missing that key ingredient left both paradigms lacking and incomplete.

What *was* it? What was missing? Nothing less than the key that unlocks the mystery, sets us free and restores *The Undying Soul* to its original position of preeminence in our lives, and of course in the lives of cancer patients—which is what I'd been after all along. What I finally realized after years of penetrating research is this: scientific atheism is founded on the belief that we can know all about the "whole" by dissecting and examining its parts. Furthermore, scientific atheism teaches us that *living* wholes, including you and me, arose on planet earth spontaneously and without external purpose, contingent on random, unpredictable, unintended physical events. By comparison, classical religion teaches us that our salvation is contingent on separating our wholeness of being into actions and events often unintended and/or beyond our control, and on the dualism that separates our bodies from our minds and our spirits.

What finally crystallized for me was that the failure of mechanistic science and the failure of classical religion *are both the result of lacking the same thing.* For each the missing ingredient is wholeness, sadly replaced by *contingency* and *separation.* The fact that this answer had been so elusive explains why the answer is so difficult to recite for you here and now.

As individuals, each of us is on our own life's journey. For most, the dangers that have haunted mankind down through the millennia—pestilence, war, and famine—have been virtually eliminated. Now, at least in modern Western society, we find ourselves facing an entirely new set of daunting challenges. Where modern science and technology have almost vanquished epidemics and starvation, they have replaced them with the heartless world of *mechanism*, that soulless world of spiritual isolation. These too are deprivations. Even though we hardly take notice, we feel it, hungering for spiritual nourishment even while our bellies stay full. We are infected with the chaos and decay of spiritual emptiness, even as we are vaccinated and take our antibiotics.

These disconnects and erosions are typically insidious, but become overwhelmingly real at the bedside of the cancer patient. When medical science has finally failed, my patients can only lie and wait. But now, *for the first time in all of human experience,* they wait without hope, without heart, tragically unaware of the reality of their undying souls.

This "immaterial" ingredient was sacrificed when we embarked on our perilous modern journey of materialism and scientific mechanism, of contingency and separateness.

There can be only one solution. At all costs, our hearts must be retrieved, and our hope must be restored. There is only one way to do this: our very souls must be rediscovered.

One day it came to me that this is what Pavel and Patricia meant when I heard them whisper, "Go back to the source, Dr. Iacoboni. Find out what's missing. Reunite ancient faith and modern science…"

Taking another long, thoughtful walk in the woods to sort this out, I let a tiny stream guide me to its hidden destination. Enveloped on all sides by enchantment and danger, darkness and rainsqualls, waterfalls and granite ledges, spectacular silent sunrises and sunsets, my mind opened to the fullness of reality that I could somehow feel more completely in the midst of the natural world. Overwhelmed by nature's intricacy and immensity, I was finally empowered to grasp the secret. While any tiny piece of the whole puzzle by itself seemed insignificant and meaningless, taken together, each leaf and petal and raindrop and pebble and twig and tree trunk and beetle and rabbit and ray of sunlight was necessary to make up the whole forest and river and meadow and thunderstorm and sunlit sky.

That was it! *That* was the answer! We have become so busy carving out our fortress in the wilderness that we have locked ourselves out of our natural birthright. We have become *so* obsessed with chopping the world up into *pieces* that we can no longer see the *whole*. Or maybe we have become so preoccupied and fascinated tinkering with the *parts* that we have forgotten about the *whole* from which they originated. Take the human genome as one example. We are constantly reminded that what we do and experience is "all because of our DNA." But DNA is just one infinitesimal molecular *piece* of a *whole* organism. In truth, there can be no DNA unless at first there is an organism that contains and produces it. A chunk of DNA in a test-tube does nothing and experiences nothing on its own. Only a *whole* organism, including of course its DNA along with hundreds of other indispensable molecular components, all working together with an *inseparable* intricacy that science still today finds inexplicable, is capable of living and experiencing.

Everything in this world can be divided into smaller component *parts*, even something as small as the atom itself. But one of the scientific breakthroughs I became aware of only later in my career, that illuminating breakthrough that changed my whole way of thinking, was the realization that a complete knowledge of the component parts of any *living* whole does not explain or predict the behavior of the intact whole. This came as a greatly surprising discovery for modern science, because modern mechanistic science is based on the belief or assumption that everything, including life, can be reduced by mechanism into its component parts. Machines can be...*because they are made by man.* Life cannot be...*because life comes from God.* And this recent discovery, although well described by modern scientists themselves, remains hotly contested and largely unaccepted by the atheist faction that dominates the discourse of modern science.

They can deny the self-evident truth all they want. But I am no longer shackled or encumbered by their self-serving need to be godless and unaccountable. Because at last in my musings, I had this final epiphany: *The Undying Soul* is the one *indivisible* whole. It alone, among all the atoms and molecules and cadavers and lab mice and tree trunks and geologic strata, cannot be carved into component parts. *The Undying Soul* alone is the singular, undisturbed, inviolate remnant of our spiritual heritage, without which we face isolation and despair. As we make our journey in life, we disregard this at our peril.

Distracted as most of us are in our hustle-and-bustle material lives, we get away with this disregard, often for years, or even decades. But the inescapable truth of the undying soul must not remain hidden when cancer strikes. Throughout the entire history of the human race, all manner of earthly tribulations such as war, pestilence, famine and floods have been endured by only one means: recognizing the very real existence of our individual undying souls.

I had made the intellectual leap. I was almost there, and there was now no turning back. Pavel and Patricia had shown me clearly what my scientific mentors didn't want me to see…what I myself refused to see for so long. What remained to make my discovery complete was to validate by repetitive observation in my clinical practice what I had thus far learned. Because this discovery doesn't turn colors in a test tube or levitate the dead. I had to be sure, because my discovery of the undying soul was to prove to be the most important thing I had ever done for anybody or for any patient…and, for that matter, for myself and all those I love.

Chapter Ten

~

ANDREW AND SARAH: IF IT'S MEANT TO BE

SARAH DROPPED BY TO SEE ME almost two years after the death of her husband, Andrew. The visit was a most welcome surprise.

Andrew had been under my care for only four months. During that time his brain tumor, a glioblastoma multiforme, progressed rapidly from its presenting symptoms. He walked into my office for our first meeting coherent, smiling, with just a "bad headache" and some tingling in his left foot. The brain scan told us why: there was a tumor in there, causing swelling and nerve damage. We went after it straightaway with stereotactic surgery, radiation, corticosteroids and chemotherapy.

Often that combination buys us at least nine to eighteen months—but not always. Despite our best efforts, Andrew went straight downhill. The cancer kept growing right on through all of our radiation and drugs. His limp rapidly turned into paralysis. His headache advanced to confusion and memory loss.

Three months after he walked into my office Andrew was bedbound, never to recover. He lingered in a coma, in his own home, for three weeks, where he finally died peacefully. Sarah and the hospice nurse were there at his bedside at the time.

Andrew's was one of the worst cases I had ever seen. The fact that he was only forty-eight years old, a loving husband and father, made it all the more tragic. What surprised me, however, was how he and Sarah went about the business of dealing with his disease almost as if it was routine. Neither one was in the medical field, so it should have been horrifying and terribly foreign. But…it wasn't.

On the other hand, it was hectic for me. Trying my best to stop Andrew's rapid decline, I was so busy with chemotherapy orders and brain scan results that I never got the chance to inquire in-depth about why they never seemed scared or worried.

As much as I'd like to be like Marcus Welby, M.D., the pace at my office is such that I am usually too consumed with the incessant demands of my practice to make house calls or even attend my patients' funerals. But for every patient of mine who died I have sent the spouse or family a personal letter of condolence. Like most surviving spouses, Sarah sent me back a nice thank-you note.

Of course, those letters and thank-you notes never say it all. I often wish I could have coffee for an hour with surviving spouses like Sarah, and I've often been told these survivors feel the same way. After so intense and personal a relationship, some in-depth closure would be welcomed by both parties. Unfortunately, from my end there is almost never time for that. New patients show up every day in extreme crisis, and it is not possible to defer the needs of the living cancer patient in order to maintain past relationships.

That fact made Sarah's unexpected drop-in visit two years after Andrew's death a real delight, especially since she came by during a rare lull in my day. Although we didn't have hours to chat, a lot was said during the short time we had. What was important to me—and to Sarah, I presumed—was to recapitulate Andrew's case with her, for the sake of closure. She listened patiently as I went on about this for just a few minutes, then she quickly changed the subject to the real purpose of this unannounced visit.

Sarah knew I would be concerned for her, after the sudden and untimely loss of her Andrew. She wanted to reassure me that she was doing well. In fact, she had sold her home and was moving her family out-of-state in order to pursue a unique business venture. She wanted me to know that her abrupt departure was due to good fortune, not from a failure to recover from her tragic loss.

I remembered that Sarah and Andrew had co-owned and operated a small business making home speaker cabinets. Now I learned that the business remained successful after Andrew's death, and was about to be acquired by a large out-of-state company. Impressed by Sarah's home-grown management and marketing skills, the new parent company had offered Sarah a management position with their office in Chicago.

Sarah was excited by the challenge, and so she accepted. What made this an even more profound life change was that she had always lived right here in North Idaho, never in a metropolis far from her family and deep social and cultural roots.

Her intrepid attitude intrigued me. It also prompted me to recall the fortitude she and Andrew displayed. At that time too, this very nice lady faced huge upheaval with extraordinary composure. Now I finally had an opportunity to discover her secret. How had she faced the terrible, incongruent tragedy of Andrew's death with so little angst? Why did she not feel any rancor towards anyone or anything? How was she self-confident enough to tackle such a huge life change, moving from her lifelong hometown, without a husband, to such a different and faraway place?

I wondered about all this, but didn't see how I could inquire about it. But that didn't matter: Sarah seemed to know what I wanted to ask. I think she sensed that I was still searching, still struggling with faith.

For doctors and scientists, the world seems so vast and complex that nothing is really simple and straightforward. Yet for Sarah it was. She took my hand, looked me squarely in the eye, and gave me her answer, simple yet profound—and unforgettable: "Things happen in our lives because they are meant to happen. My move to the big city will work out, if it's meant to be."

These were not just hopeful words. I could feel her deep conviction, immersed in a peaceful calm. Indeed, I found myself moved by her sheer certainty. Speechless for the moment, I returned her steady gaze in grateful stunned silence. Then she patted my hands and we both nodded, got up and embraced in friendship and caring.

When Sarah left I sat back in my office chair for a good while, ignoring the calls and pages. I had to take it all in. For many more moments I felt just a bit overwhelmed, as I pondered her sage pronouncement.

The full impact of Sarah's wisdom has come to me slowly but steadily over time. In her simple statement she drew the line between all that is faith and all that denies it. Her response captured the very essence of faith itself.

For Sarah, her husband's death was not bewildering. Like all the important life events she experienced, her husband's passing was preordained, so there was nothing at all mysterious about it. Quite simply, Sarah had never gone down the path of scientific atheism or moral relativism.

For those with Sarah's faith there are no existential mysteries, not even cancer itself. The only mystery for her is that manifest by God and His creation—a grandeur that made her life vibrant and wonderful. She believed all lives are tended, and intended, by a Supreme Being, and that His care encompasses all the major events of those lives, including her husband's death, and now this move across the country.

The one simple concept that Sarah so poignantly demonstrated to me, not just with words but with impeccable action, is at the core of the dilemma for cancer patients: the core conflict between ancient faith and modern science. It is this conflict, where there should be none, which has all too often banished the undying soul from daily awareness.

The belief that now dominates modern scientific discourse is that all observable entities, including life itself, and even human consciousness, came into being contingent upon innumerable preceding *random* material events. In other words, life as we know it was never "meant to be," as Sarah put it. Evolution could have stopped with squid, or pigs or apes, or Neanderthal Man. In this paradigm, the emergence of *Homo sapiens* was as much an accident of nature as was the formation of the first living cell four billion years ago. The odds against it all were preposterously enormous, yet like a 300 million-to-one lottery ticket, someone had to randomly win. Life just turned out the way it did… randomly. By accident. It was never actually meant to be just so.

This means that nothing in life—not even our own lives, for that matter—was ever "intended" by a Higher Power. The universe came into being with the explosion of the Big Bang some fifteen billion years ago, and somewhere in the unfathomable immensity of limitless galaxies was one planet 93 million miles from its star. Carbon and hydrogen and oxygen and nitrogen were unleashed from the other primordial elements on this planet, and after a billion years of random molecular collisions, carbon-based life forms somehow (no one has any precise idea how) came into being. These single-celled organisms grew, became more complex, and organized themselves into very simple multi-cellular organisms, which eventually morphed, randomly, into ever more complex creatures over time. Then later, along came plants and insects, then dinosaurs, fishes, birds and finally mammals. At the end of this evolutionary journey came the most complex creature of all, *Homo sapiens*.

One famous member of the species *Homo sapiens* was Charles Darwin, who spent most of his life as a faithful Christian, and eventually made one of the most famous scientific discoveries of all time. While it was Darwin's faith that inspired him to study nature and discover its God-given laws of behavior, what he found was quite at variance with the conventional church dogma of the late 1800's.

The prevailing late-nineteenth-century biblical interpretation was that all the species on the planet, including man, had existed unchanged since Genesis. We now know that's not true—that dinosaurs, wooly mammoths, saber-toothed tigers and so on—on and on—once lived and are now gone. In fact, it had been known for over fifty years before Darwin that life forms were changing, albeit very slowly, over vast stretches of time. Darwin's theory specified the cause for this observation: the "fittest" members of any species would survive over time due to a process that he called "natural selection." The process of "artificial selection" had already been demonstrated to Darwin by ranchers and breeders of livestock, who had intentionally culled herds and chosen animals for specific traits over successive generations of "selective" breeding. You don't think there were ever any Guernsey cows or poodles existing successfully in the wild before they were bred into their present form, do you?

The huge difference between what had been known for centuries by ranchers and what Darwin claimed was this: Darwin said that over vast stretches of time, not only would traits change *within* a species, but that eventually whole *new* species would emerge from the old. This is the process we call "evolution."

The question ever since Darwin has been "How? How do living things *change* their 'fitness' in order to survive the gauntlet of natural selection and eventually evolve?" It's easy to understand how dogs and cattle and horses are selectively bred by the directing influence of the breeder, who is *intelligently designing* the process. Some horses are bred for speed, others for pulling wagons. Some dogs are bred for personal protection, others for hounding game. What, if any, directing influence is responsible for fish becoming reptiles or mice becoming dogs, and in particular, for the emergence of *Homo sapiens* from the primordial soup?

Darwin's *On the Origin of Species* disturbed established religions because of his theory of new species, including man himself, emerging anew over time. *Long* periods of time: study of the fossil record clearly reveals that life has existed for four *billion* years, that vertebrates emerged about 500 million years ago, and mammals arose 90 million years ago. Pre-human hominids emerged about seven million years ago, *Homo sapiens* appeared about 200 thousand years back…and it's only in about the last 5000 years that the human race has been what we now consider "civilized."

We all know about change. We all know how different the human experience is today compared to yesterday. Electricity was invented 100 years ago. Before then there were only lanterns, candles and wood stoves. Paved roads and cars became prevalent only sixty years ago. Before that there were trains, wagons and horses. Color television has only been around since about 1970, personal computers and cell phones since 1995. The global Internet has been part of the human experience for less than a generation, though most people under the age of thirty can't imagine a world without cyberspace.

All these progressions in human civilization, from spears to carts to houses to roads to trains to cars to jet-planes to refrigerators to super-computers, were intelligently designed by human inventors. Keeping food cold with mere electricity required a lot of engineering, but no more iceboxes please.

Because we humans are the cause of these technological and societal changes, most non-scientists tend to think of organic evolution in the same way: as the result of some intended plan orchestrated by a design-ing intellect, more or less in the same way as human invention.

And so what about the most complex entity on Earth, life itself? Is there a God who planned it? Was it "all meant to be," as Sarah told me? Or was it never intended or designed by any omniscient intellect?

That is the ultimate question. It is not just a line in the sand— it is an impassable divide. On one side is ancient faith. On the other side is the dogma of scientific materialism. The side of faith affirms the real-ity of the soul. On the other side is a world without ultimate meaning, without sacredness or spiritual wholes.

Most religions don't pretend to know how hominids turned into humans. That's what religion refers to as "the great mystery of life," necessitating no other "factual" explanation. All religion says is "God did it."

Scientists, on the other hand, always search for a rational explanation to understand the events that take place in our world. This has been a noble and honest goal, driven for two thousand years by the belief that the laws of nature discovered by scientists were an approximation of the true laws designed by the Creator.

Throughout the twentieth century, however, science has gradually moved away from this foundational belief, and has attempted to become autonomous from any supernatural influence like a creating God. But it seems to me that we scientists are making the biggest mistake possible by asserting that we can explain away life itself purely by scientific mechanisms.

Explanations of the workings of the natural world—the how and the why—are rightfully left to science. But when scientists of the latter twentieth century went looking for a self-organizing force in the biosphere that would have preordained the emergence of life—the how and the why—they couldn't find it. Absent precise evidence of this force, these researchers took the easy way out. They simply declared it didn't exist…

Let me emphasize that. Because scientists couldn't find and identify this force, they declared it didn't exist…and from that "finding" concluded that life on Earth is accidental, ergo unintended, ergo never meant to be. If our lives are truly unintended, truly accidental, and not designed by an Intelligent Creator, then all ancient faith is swept away with this one bold proclamation. Along with this goes belief in the soul.

At this point it's fair to ask…*do* we have an undying soul? Or is what I'm describing mere fantasy? For me, the question is as follows: Is there hope for my afflicted patients beyond what remedies modern pharmaceuticals can provide?

To find your answer, you might start by taking a walk in the woods. Let the wind stir up your ancient senses. After you are refreshed, I beg that you keep reading.

And so you will, *if it is meant to be.*

Chapter Eleven

⟿

TERRI: FACING DEATH WITH LOVE

THE DAY CAME WHEN I DISCOVERED that Terri's cancer had spread to her liver in an aggressive fashion. I had to tell her that night in her hospital room, while she lay in bed surrounded by her sons and daughters.

Terri and her family all broke down in tears. I suspected their disappointment was particularly intense because just three months earlier I had told Terri she was in remission.

Before that, Terri had courageously endured six months of intensive chemotherapy fighting her lung cancer. Because she had an advanced case when diagnosed, the odds against success were long. But we worked through a number of complications together, and got her through.

Now…

Delivering terrible news is never easy for me, no matter how often I've been required to do so. Even so, I was surprised how low I felt telling Terri. Of course I found myself second-guessing. Maybe I shouldn't have put her through all that. Why couldn't I have left her alone from the beginning? I raised her hopes, only to dash them all to bits. What kind of a doctor was I, putting her through all that for nothing? So happy and proud of myself just three short months ago and here she was back in the hospital, dying. What must her family think of me?

I stood with her adult children gathered at her bedside. While they hadn't been much involved during her courses of chemotherapy, and none had been present when Terri told me to fight her cancer "full-force," now they rallied around. I told myself I would understand if they were angry. While I had certainly done my best, that's not always something a grieving family can grasp.

Not long after I wrote the "Do Not Resuscitate" order in Terri's hospital chart, her son asked to speak to me. He hadn't been to any of her office visits, so I had no idea what he was thinking; neither did the nurses who relayed his request. So I braced myself when I went to greet him in the hallway outside Terri's room. Already feeling down about her condition, I half-expected him to stand there and second-guess me. I knew I'd have no answer because in the end all I could do was not enough.

He was teary-eyed. To my surprise, he extended his hand and gave me a warm, firm handshake. "I just wanted you to know, doctor, that Mom says that she loves you, and she's so grateful for all you've done. She wanted me to be sure and tell you that."

Surprise, sorrow: I was almost overcome by his words. "She loves you" is not something many patients say about their doctors, especially after such bad news.

We consoled each other as best we could, murmuring quietly. But as I recovered myself, even as I turned to walk away, I found myself filled with unexpected warmth. A feeling of...renewal, accompanied by a thought:

This is why I do what I do. It's for moments like these.

I felt this way because Terri's expression of gratitude and love was the sweetest victory of all, the holy grail of human experience: the triumph over fear of death. Some people climb impossible mountain peaks, jump out of airplanes and engage in other risky adventures, in order to stare death in the face, and live. But Terri had done much more. She accepted that death had won, and was going willingly, with grace and expressions of love.

Which brings us back to what I said earlier about the essential meaning of life.

My belief is that you can never uncover the mystery of life until you decide for yourself whether all life, indeed your own life, is *contingent* (accidental) or *designed* (intended). The answer boils down entirely to the "randomness/accidental" model versus the "designed/wholeness" vision.

On their deathbeds, many of my dear patients wonder, often silently, and even sometimes aloud, if their lives have eternal meaning. Does a spirit world await them upon their passing? Or will they simply be dispatched to some final trash heap, withering into dust along with all the other used-up, randomly assembled and soulless creatures of planet earth? For all the preceding millennia of human existence, the dying never had to face such profoundly disturbing questions. Now this terrible burden has been imposed upon them by the rising tide of the modern secular movement, whose message echoes the mantra of mainstream modern science: life on earth is merely the result of an enormously improbable cosmic accident, *contingent* upon *random*, purposeless chemical reactions that were never *intended* or designed by a Creator.

But I do not believe this is so. What I have discovered on my search is that "Ashes to Ashes, Dust to Dust" applies only to flesh, not to our resilient, immortal, undying souls. And this message is what must be delivered to the bedside of the dying, as well as into the oncology clinic, those sacred spaces I am so privileged to visit, every day and every night.

Chapter Twelve

⁓

MARIA

MARIA WAS A NATIVE OF PORTUGAL, born in the Azores. Eventually she moved to New York City, where she enjoyed a new and exciting cosmopolitan life. But eventually the excitement of city life lost its luster for her, especially after she met Matthew, the man who was to become her husband. Skilled with his hands and good-hearted, his desire was to marry Maria and raise a family far from the hustle and bustle of a big city. Together they ended up about as far away as they could get from Manhattan, making their home in a woodsy northern Idaho town ten miles from the Canadian border.

Maria had been settled in Idaho for about twelve years, with a family growing up around her, when she developed a lump in her breast that turned out to be cancer. At that time three years ago, she initially saw one of my partners, who advised her to undergo chemotherapy as an "adjuvant" precautionary treatment. The idea of chemotherapy didn't sit well with her. She protested, but after much insistence from my colleague Maria gave it a try. It made her ill and depressed; she hated it. Unsure what to do next, she sought my opinion.

From the moment I met her, Maria enchanted me. She had a spirit so earthy and moving that she held me spellbound, in an endearing, nurturing sort of way. Perhaps a stranger might find her plain-looking, even homely. In a word I found her lovable, and we two formed an intense bond, like brother and sister, not long after we met.

I could see it was senseless to force this lovely character into doing something she could not abide. In any case, she had no active disease so the chemo was only a precaution. I told her it was okay to stop treatment.

Since Maria wasn't getting chemo she didn't need to see me often, just every six months for a routine check-up and mammograms. Whenever we met it was a special occasion, and I always had a hard time getting out of her exam room and on to other patients.

Thirty months passed this way. Then, four months after our last visit, I got a call from her family doctor who cared for her in her hometown sixty miles north. "Maria's blood's not right Steve. Maybe you'd better see her pretty soon to figure this out." That I did, and my worst fears were confirmed.

Breast cancer was the least of our worries. Maria had now developed acute leukemia.

Just as before, Maria refused to take chemotherapy. "Those chemicals don't agree with my body," she said. "Why can't I just try some herbs?" "It's different this time, Maria," I told her. "Without chemo, this leukemia will kill you." "Well then so be it," she replied, "I've lived a full life, and I just can't put myself through that again…"

We were stuck. What could I do?

I knew that Maria was very involved with her church and had become a deeply devout Catholic. So I tried a different approach. I intuited that my only hope for convincing Maria to go far beyond her comfort zone and consider chemotherapy was to do the same myself… even if that meant pushing the boundaries of patient-physician dialogue. To this day, I remember vividly my hesitation as I contemplated my approach. But I was desperate to find a way to convince her. It was my solemn duty as her physician to do all that I could to help her. Besides that, we had formed a close-knit bond. I knew that I could speak to her in a way that might only be allowed between two souls who knew, trusted and respected each other. So I ventured, "Maria, don't you think you're being a little selfish? If you let yourself go you'll be abandoning your husband and your children. Do you think Jesus would approve of that? Do you think Jesus let you get leukemia just so you could give up and die?"

I knew as I said these words that I was stepping squarely into her very personal territory. These weren't Sunday-sermon cautions to an ambivalent Christian who went to church only on Christmas and Easter: I'd thrown down the gauntlet to a True Believer. How would she respond?

My entreaty to Maria was not based on logic, but I knew by now that many things about being a cancer doctor went far beyond reason itself. As the great theologian Saint Thomas Aquinas himself asserted long ago, reason is superceded by faith. And my own experience in the mystical realm of oncology likewise taught me this very same thing.

When a doctor spends decades in practice, even the most complicated cancer cases become intellectually routine. But *solving* these cases requires the soulful doctor to go way beyond the merely intellectual. Like a professional athlete who goes out to play his two hundredth game, a doctor's performance is only partly dependent on well-learned facts and skills. He has to have *heart* in order to excel. No amount of factual knowledge by itself would have been enough to allow me to say what I dared to say to Maria. But as I said, I had learned to love soulful Maria...so I spoke to her from my heart, more as a family member than as an authoritative white-coat making a cold, statistical prognostication.

With another patient my approach might have been out of bounds, unappreciated or ineffective. Not with Maria. We had something vitally important in common.

By the time I "chastised" Maria I'd been transformed: I was, like her, a true believer...in the power of faith. I wasn't just manipulating her to get my way. I sincerely believed that my provocative inquiry was valid. A doctor can't formulate such questions unless he understands his patient well enough to know what he or she truly cares about. Furthermore, a doctor can't ask so boldly, in the professional setting, without knowing that patient well enough to trust that she or he will find the questions appropriate. It's only intimate knowledge that justifies the risks and potential rewards available to a doctor when he or she works from the heart and *beyond* facts or reason.

With Maria, my heartfelt plea for her to reconsider was received in kind. No appeal to her intellect could overrule what her heart told her. She could not ignore such an explicit request spoken from a source she believed to be sincere. I was, after all, the doctor who had cut short her chemo two-and-a-half years ago. If I had supported her wish to avoid the awful chemo back then, then she could trust me now when I was compelled to recommend it.

In the deeply emotional conversation that followed, Maria admitted that even something as onerous as chemo might be made bearable, *if* she knew her doctor cared about her as much as I did.

She agreed to proceed, as difficult as that was—and difficult hardly describes it.

The chemotherapy we use to treat adult acute leukemia is so harsh that patients must be hospitalized for weeks to receive it. That hasn't been the case for most other chemo regimens for almost fifteen years now. These days almost ninety percent of all chemotherapy can be safely administered in the outpatient setting.

But not for acute leukemia. The reason is simple: the treatment target is the white blood cell itself—the most chemo-sensitive cell in the body. These tiny warriors form the core of the human immune system, yet are also the cells most vulnerable to collateral damage when chemotherapy is administered. Damage done by chemotherapy to these white blood cells is the reason why all cancer patients are warned about the risk of infection following treatment. To destroy cancers we must also kill millions of white bloods cells, weakening the body's immune defenses.

That's all bad enough. But when we give chemotherapy to a leukemia patient, as opposed to say a patient with colon cancer, killing white blood cells is our intent, not just unfortunate collateral damage. In order to defeat acute leukemia we have no choice: we must open fire with an overwhelming barrage, and maintain a fierce chemotherapy assault long enough to entirely eliminate the malignant leukemic clone.

By the time we're done we've annihilated 99.99 percent of the patient's circulating white blood cells. That leaves the patient's immune system severely weakened, requiring a prolonged and dangerous recovery phase. It is during this two-to-three-week recovery period when the patient is most likely to perish, from bleeding or infection or both. Every day the patient remains in this extremely vulnerable state could be their last, if infection strikes or a blood vessel ruptures.

Sounds gruesome, I know. But the fact is that in many cases this strategy works. This grim approach has been the standard routine for about thirty-five years; exhaustive research over all those years has failed to discover a superior treatment regimen. Fortunately, the time, effort, risk and suffering frequently pay off: the remission rate for leukemia with this strenuous method turns out to be a very respectable 60-70 percent.

Pretty awesome really, when you realize that *failing* to achieve remission *always* results in death.

All that said…I'll never forget how difficult it was for me to ask Maria to commit to this long ordeal. Although I proposed the undertaking with all the sincerity I could muster, my rational side kept bringing up all the obvious medical contingencies that come along with such a gamble. *What if it fails? What if it provokes serious complications that result in an even longer, more painful hospital stay? Bleeding, infection, stroke...what if...what if...what if?*

Out of my professional obligation, I presented to Maria the darker side of the treatment scenario. I left nothing out, and still I remember that as I spoke, I listened to myself with some disbelief. *"Maria, you'll never go for this,"* I thought while describing the potential perils and pain. *"You wouldn't tolerate a simple breast cancer regimen, so how can I hope to convince you to submit to all this...? But...I want you to try, because I want you to live."*

Only later did I realize that fear of death had nothing to do with her decision.

Throughout my long dissertation Maria stared at me in silence, her eyes piercing into mine. She did not stop me to ask the usual questions about "odds" and "what ifs." She simply listened, although so intently that I could feel her stare reading my heart, penetrating through to my soul. When I was finally finished, she nodded. "Very well, Dr Iacoboni." she said evenly. "I trust you, and I'll do as you say. I'll take the chemo. When do you want me to start?"

That was it. Maria, the same lady who wouldn't sit still in the chemo chair for four hours of preventative treatments per month for breast cancer...was now willing to enter the hospital for over four weeks.

This was wonderful—I hoped. But...why? Why did Maria agree?

It took me a while to learn the answer. When I did at last, it's only because I was listening to a language Maria heard while listening to me, a resonance that begs understanding beyond words.

Maria had eliminated all contingencies. She had given up control to an absolute Higher Power; the outcome would be what it would be. Facing the life and death battle about to begin, she maintained her spiritual equilibrium by manifesting perfect faith, free of reservations. She would not try to maintain control by *bargaining with God.*

Maria had solved the mystery of cancer without ever contemplating physiology or pharmacology. She understood that the real "answer" to cancer was, like life itself, understood by the heart, not the intellect. This she accomplished by adopting a contingency-free perspective. To approach the world in this way, to be free of self-centered thoughts, and to readily give up all the doubts inherent in day to day living requires only one thing: faith. The kind of faith that is utterly free of contingencies.

Maria entered the hospital near death from her leukemia. She stayed the four weeks we had planned, then two more before her recovery from the high-dose chemo was complete—a month and a half in the hospital! She had many, many long, difficult days and nights. Her throat was swollen red and raw to the point that she could barely swallow. Her skin turned white from lack of red blood cells. Constant diarrhea made bowel movements so painful for her that we had to give her morphine. By the end of the chemo she was so depleted we had to feed her intravenously and transfuse blood and platelets daily.

Every day her family visited, and I tried my best to console and encourage them. Her sisters came from New York City, full of questions, terribly worried and brimming with "what-ifs?"(contingencies). Every day I told them I could not predict the outcome for Maria, beyond that which was already so brutally obvious: she would experience remission, and live; or die, from infection, bleeding or persistent leukemia. Day after day for forty days we had the same painful conversation.

All the while Maria said little. Of course, I had to know what she was feeling physically so that I could prescribe the appropriate medical remedies, but she described her ailments only because I asked. In all that time she never asked me whether she was going to "make it."

She never questioned her decision to accept and endure such an ordeal, with no guarantees of a favorable outcome. She demonstrated a patience and perseverance that was truly on a par with the saintliness of Pavel and Patricia.

Throughout that time I struggled to maintain clinical objectivity—detachment. But with every passing day that saw her survive into the next, I found new reason to believe. Despite all the inherent risks and dangers, maybe she just might make it.

Somehow, Maria had infused me with her uncompromising faith. Even when she was very sick, with a high fever and no white blood cells, neither one of us was really worried. I had never before felt that kind of magical optimism. Maria willed it upon herself, and into me.

Then on the forty-second day after Maria came into the hospital, she walked out. Her leukemia had been vanquished. The arduous chemo worked. From the very first day, Maria knew she would walk away. And she did.

The nursing staff called it a miracle, and proclaimed it my finest hour on our cancer ward. Everyone who met and worked with Maria had fallen in love with her and had worried over her fate. All I could do was tell them to do what I myself was doing: hope and pray. Every day we talked about Maria. Every day we prayed for Maria. We were still stuck to some extent on contingencies, preoccupied with which way it would go. When Maria achieved her remission, and left the hospital to return home robust and in full health, it was as if she had broken free, escaping some brutal incarceration. It felt as if she had liberated all of us as well.

What I did not fully comprehend at the time, but realize now, is that once Maria had made up her mind and settled on having the treatment, she had unconditionally accepted the outcome, without fear or attachment to her survival—though she of course did want to survive. She just knew this was out of her hands, and with great grace gave up trying to be in control.

Only much later, as I reflected on Maria's inspirational return to health, did I begin to see how the essence of her triumph shared something achieved by Pavel, Sarah, Patricia and Clarence, despite their different outcomes. Only then did I start to understand what all these "angels" had taught me. I recognized at last what they intuitively knew: that the key to the mystery of cancer is spiritual wholeness, manifested by perfect faith, free of any and all contingencies.

From that wholeness of spirit and freedom from doubt…opens the doorway to…

…*The Undying Soul.*

Chapter Thirteen

⌒

TALES OF TRIUMPH

A TYPICALLY BUSY CLINIC DAY ends with me seated leaning back in my old office chair, and let me confess that after ten action-packed hours seeing cancer patients, my desk is a mess. Accumulated lab reports, CAT scans, phone messages, prescriptions to write, follow-up phone call requests: all these pile up. Once all the patients have come and gone, I still have several hours of paperwork to wade through before I get to head home.

When the clinic is quiet at day's end, I pause and take a moment to reflect on what all happened through the workday. The fact is that every day in an oncologist's office is full of drama: for the doctor, but of course, far more so for the patients and their families. So as I stare wistfully at the artwork or at the ceiling during this one moment of quiet solitude, I have a chance to gather my thoughts and process my emotions. It may surprise you to learn that my predominant mindset is by no means one of sadness or defeat. Quite to the contrary: it is one of triumph.

I have told you stories of people who faced imminent death by cancer with grace and courage. Some lost their battle, but won the war by dying "a good death." But there are also so many others, like Maria, who were victorious at earning a second chance at life. These are my patients in remission, who come to see me once every three to six months for their routine check-ups.

Let me introduce you to few of these, whose successes are most instructive.

An Unknown Ingredient

I presented Nathan's case to the "university hotline" consultant over the phone.

"He's going to die," was the terse response.

The phone consult was Nathan's idea, which he urged me to pursue right after our first meeting, during which I'd told him his prognosis was bleak. Nathan wanted to get a second, "hotline" opinion from a "hotline university." Now he had one—or I did, at my end of the phone—and the expert opinion was that his case was terminal.

But Nathan didn't die after-all. That awkward phone conversation took place five years ago, and today in my office Nathan and I celebrated his unlikely survival.

"I don't know how we did it, Doc," he said. Everybody told me I was a goner, except you. You saved my life, and I can't thank you enough."

Perhaps so. But since the honest truth is that I don't quite know how we managed to prevent Nathan's cancer from growing and spreading, I just nodded meekly, trying again not to let on that I too was mystified by our success.

There are many times in the life of a physician when things go wrong and you don't know why, which makes those situations all the more difficult. It's the hardest thing to tell a patient and their family that you just don't know the reason their cancer won't respond to the treatment, why they are so sick, or even why they have to die. Such is the nature of cancer medicine, however. I'm grateful that my patients have never blamed me, no matter how devastated they were, and that their families have almost always tried to be gracious even in their grief.

With Nathan, that table was turned, however—at least in one sense. He continued to thrive, enjoying a prolonged remission *with no obvious explanation I could discern.* Happily, in such a positive situation, I was under no pressure to provide one. Who cares how you hit the game-winning home run? The ball went over the centerfield fence and that's all that matters.

What did happen in Nathan's case? Was it just luck?

Doctors are taught to be naturally curious, to learn from every unique clinical experience, good or bad. For five years with Nathan I waited for the other shoe to drop, but it never did. Finally I stopped waiting for the worst and instead began searching for a plausible reason—presuming any existed.

To be sure, my recollection of those turbulent early interactions with Nathan remain vivid.

Nathan had prostate cancer, which is not uncommon among men in their later years, say in the eighth decade and beyond. But Nathan got the disease at the relatively tender age of fort-eight. Not only that, his case was bad: when diagnosed, the cancer was already widespread, eating into the bones of his hips and spine. No wonder my phone consultant "expert" was pessimistic.

Did I mention that Nathan could not hear that "expert's" end of that conversation? And of course he was anxious to learn what was said. Stumbling a little over my words, I muttered, "He, um, sort of said what I said ... and...said I was doing all that he would do, so we just have to hope for the best."

I suppose I made up that last little bit about hope, but only because *I* had some, so Nathan deserved to feel it.

A Very Squeaky Wheel

Not that hope soothed him. Nathan was frantic. In fact, I can safely say that he was the most frantic patient I've cared for in twenty-five years of doctoring. "I've got a wife!" he shouted. "Kids! I own a business! I can't die now Dr. Iacoboni, I just can't!"

When patients rant in this fashion, they usually do so just a few times, then take a softer, less desperate approach as we settle down to the business of treatment. But not Nathan. I saw him once a week for almost two months straight, sometimes twice a week early on, always confronting the same, emotion-loaded conversation: "You gotta cure me, Dr Iacoboni, you've just got to! I can't die! How much time do I really have? Can't you do *something?!*"

Every visit, I gave Nathan the same answer, the one that I had learned from my professors at MD Anderson—yes, the very reassurance I'd considered deceptively optimistic. Yet here I was echoing their teaching.

"I don't know how long you have to live Nathan; no one does. Don't worry so much about the statistics. *You* are a statistic of *one,* my friend, and that's just how we're going to approach this. Give the treatment a chance to work. That, more than anything, will determine your fate."

Honestly, these sessions felt more like emotional therapy than oncology discussions. They always began with Nathan finding something to fiddle with in the exam room, usually a paper towel or an exam glove he'd taken out of the drawer, He would twist it nervously, staring out the window, rarely making eye contact except when he would suddenly cry, "Gawd-damnit Doc. You gotta fix this!!"

"Yes, Nathan. Give the treatment a chance to work. Remember you're a statistic of one…"

Nathan would depart only a little less anxious. Often, I think he only left my office because we'd exhausted each other.

And he exhausted not just the two of us: in the year it took Nathan to "settle down" he drove my nurses and secretaries crazy. Immediately after offering therapy to him, I'd have to perform another session with staff—he really was one in 10,000, not somebody they were prepared to deal with on a regular basis. I give them a lot of credit for being so patient with Nathan, addressing demands that were above and beyond, doing their best to minister to his vast assortment of needs. Even with their best efforts and mine, it took about a year for Nathan to stop asking, every visit, "When am I going to die?"

All that aside, I must give credit where credit is due. Nathan took his meds regularly. Not only that, he kept working more than fulltime. An electrician and owner of his own business, he was fantastically successful partly because of his frenetic and compulsive nature.

Years continued to pass without the expected disease progression. Nathan's urologist expressed astonishment, remarking that I was some kind of miracle worker, though we both knew I had not done anything extraordinary to treat Nathan, other than soothe him somewhat, week after week.

Or *was* that it after all? I wondered. These lengthy visits, a regimen of sorts, each aimed at providing a larger measure of comfort and reassurance than a typical schedule would allow during a brief monthly chat…could they have made a crucial difference?

Of course I still don't know. Maybe it was Nathan himself, in all his desperate determination to live, though I've described equally determined, if not so frantic patients who didn't make it.

Deep down, though, I don't think his frenetic near-hysteria did him much good, if any at all; it consumed so much time and energy that it often got in the way of his chemotherapy. I actually was concerned for a long time that Nathan was going to worry himself to death. In other words, I thought his indulgences were more harmful than helpful to him, and I certainly don't recommend Nathan's behavior as some kind of remedy. I give to each patient according to their needs, usually for more down to earth reasons like uncontrolled pain, or lack of functional abilities like not eating, shortness of breath, etc. My goal is to see each as often as they need to see me and offer encouragement along the way, but I don't want them spending more time in my office than necessary; after all, they still have a life to live and enjoy.

Probably Nathan's success resulted from that simple yet sublime element that underpins all of medicine: a profound bond between doctor and patient, united against all odds, facing the difficulty of the situation together, no matter what the outcome may turn out to be.

Then There Is Jan...

It's always a special day when Jan comes in.

Four years ago she had advanced ovarian cancer. That means the statistical odds she would be alive to bring me cookies today were less than one in fifty. Nowadays, I have to force myself to find time among hugs, deer-hunting stories and pictures of grandchildren to actually listen to her lungs, examine her abdomen and review her lab work and X-rays.

Hugs are special. I amazed one of my older mentors one day while we were chatting, by remarking that I count it a "good day" when I receive five hugs or more, and Jan's are great.

That's not all that's great about her. I clearly recall the steadfast courage and confidence she displayed during those challenging days when exploratory surgery revealed her dreadful diagnosis, followed by the months of "no promises" chemotherapy that followed.

All through that, Jan was never bitter or sad. She trusted me and the Lord that she'd make it through.

Make it she did. And sometime after the treatment succeeded, Jan invited me to visit her and her husband out at their ranch. I gladly accepted. I was ready for a little downtime, and there's nothing like a day in the country to warm the soul.

I found her in the kitchen peeling fresh apples from their own orchard that were soon to be made into homemade pie for our evening dessert. I savored the smells while watching her work, the kind of scene I just don't get to see often enough…

Suddenly Jan turned, rushing into a story that must have been on her mind for a very long time—the kind of thing that a doctor almost never hears.

She started by describing that period of time soon before I met her. Jan had spent a week in the hospital getting intravenous nutrition and medication, recovering from the procedure that established her devastating diagnosis. After the operation her surgeon, a kind and dedicated man, told her that he was unable to remove all the cancer, and that therefore "she probably only had only one Christmas left." Following that came another week of recovery while Jan lay in bed out there on her ranch, waiting to see if a doctor at our cancer center would try to save her life.

You can imagine how awful that kind of waiting might be. Toward the end, fear, grief and regrets overwhelmed her.

Bill, her devoted husband of thirty-five years, found her curled on the couch, weeping inconsolably. "What's wrong honey?" she remembers him asking.

"I told him," Jan said to me in her bright kitchen. "I told him, 'The surgeon says I'm not gonna make it. He says he's not sure if the chemo is even going to do me any good. Maybe I should just give up.'"

Jan paused with her hands poised above the flour. "Doctor Iacoboni? Do you know what Bill said to me, right then and there? He stood up, looked at me and said, 'Well, just go ahead and die then, you big crybaby. Never mind that you'll be leaving me and the kids and grandkids alone without you. The hell with it, if you're gonna be this way. Is the only person you care about just yourself? I mean it, godammit! I want to know right here and now what you intend to do, fight or give up!'"

Jan remembers how a quiver in Bill's lower lip betrayed him even as he groused at her. The prospect of his lifetime mate abandoning him without a fight was more than he could bear. The fear of abandonment and loneliness soon overwhelmed him, and after he said his piece he collapsed into her arms. "We wailed and hugged for at least five whole minutes before settling down." Jan continued. "I knew right then and there that I had to fight with everything I had. This cancer was *only* going to beat me if it *could*, not because I *let* it."

So *that* was why she was so strong throughout it all.

Strength was part of it. But was it her will to live that helped her beat the odds? Or love for her husband, himself a strong man, and proud… who couldn't live one day without her?

You tell me, folks, 'cause right now the Lord only knows. I just thank Him for the privilege of knowing and caring for all the 'Jans' in my practice.

…and Dina

"I got to meet Katie Couric, Dr. Iacoboni! Look here's a picture of the two of us together."

Dina was diagnosed with pancreas cancer fully five years ago. It was inoperable. The Virginia Mason Medical Center in Seattle had a promising new protocol for this unyielding disease, so I sent her there for a consult. They were able to supply me with the investigational materials and protocol that allowed Dina to receive treatment here in her hometown, rather than 400 miles away.

To our mutual surprise and wonderment, Jan's cancer began shrinking. After three months on trial, the tumor was small enough that I could send her back to the surgeon to have what little was left surgically removed.

Dina recovered from surgery remarkably well. All the *visible* cancer in her was now gone. But cancer specialists know all too well that cancer is a microscopic disease, and that a surgical "remission" is no guarantee that it won't come back. In her case a relapse was virtually a certainty.

Six months later I got a call from Dina that I feared spelled the beginning of the end: she was vomiting blood. I had her rushed to the hospital, frankly expecting the worst. But when my gastroenterologist colleague passed the endoscope down into her stomach, all he found was a routine ulcer, not a big new cancer eroding through the stomach wall. Dina healed up nicely from that, and was back home in three days.

I shook my head as she left the hospital that time, still convinced that she'd be back before long, with a problem that wouldn't be as easy to remedy.

For two years there were none. And because two years is like an eternity of survival for pancreatic cancer, Dina was officially declared a "survivor." With that distinction came an invitation to a survivor's soiree in San Francisco, attended by such celebrities as Katie Couric, whose first husband died from colon cancer at an early age.

I saw Dina in follow-up every three months, and each time she exhibited no signs of recurrence. Finally however, the inevitable did occur. She had a new spot on her lung and it was growing.

This discovery led to an intense debate between me and those doctors in Seattle. They were still following her because she'd been treated on their protocol. In response to this relapse, they recommended giving her more chemo. My intuition told me we should do surgery instead.

Intuition? I let a patient's life depend upon something as vague as that?

Perhaps I'd better define what I mean.

Practice and Intuition

The life of a physician is one of *practice*. Practicing for what? To get better through experience and repetition. The word "practice" really is appropriate, even though most of us don't commonly compare athletics to medicine. Yet in a very real sense athletes and doctors are doing what they do in much the same way: *gaining competence through repetition of a highly complex skill set whose mastery defies straightforward explanation.*

Most people understand how that works on the playing field. Whenever a pitcher or a batter or a basketball player or a quarterback has an exceptional game, spectators and analysts alike expend enormous effort trying to figure out what made their play so great on that occasion. After all, the goal is to have *more* great games, right? Sometimes you can look back at the game films and notice that the homerun resulted from a small but definite change in batting stance or the way a hitter swings the bat.

Often, however, the analysis gets stuck in endless debate. And that's because so many times the defining difference between success and failure remains elusive.

As the great Michael Jordan said after he made his comeback, "I just had to find my rhythm." In much the same way, a seasoned older doctor might sidestep logic when explaining his or her success with the chosen procedure by simply saying, "I just had an intuition."

So I took a stand for Dina, based on intuition rather than logic, and she accepted my recommendation over that of my university colleagues.

Dina underwent the surgery and got through it without much difficulty. All the visible cancer was again removed, but what would happen next?

I kept a careful watch over her, and sure enough, six months later another lung nodule popped up. This came as no big surprise…to me.

After all, I wasn't naive enough to think that the first lung operation would be the end of it.

But what about Dina? Would this latest failure cause her to lose faith in me?

That's another aspect of a doctor's intuition. You have to understand your patient, including the kinds of challenges they will or will not tolerate. You have to intuit the disease…*within the larger context of the patient as a whole.*

Medical science always tries to separate the two. That's why most doctors have trouble exercising intuition: it violates their educational foundation. But I knew my Dina. When I told her there would have to be another operation, she just said, "Okay, whatever you say." Dina trusted me implicitly with her life, and for that I was immensely grateful.

Dina survived the second lung operation, which was no small feat. In fact, as I had expected, she sailed right through it.

Now we're five years on, and there has been no more activity of her cancer – a cancer that by all odds should have taken her from us long ago.

I saw Dina for a four-month check-up and again gave her the all-clear. After that great news, I also told her that, in all honesty, I really couldn't understand why she had beaten the odds.

Dina leaned back in her chair and gave me a warm smile. "I know why. I've got a great doctor." Then she laughed as she stood up.

With that we hugged and she headed out the door, back to her life.

So you see, my life as a cancer doctor, as painful as it can be sometimes, is also filled with much joy. Miracles like this happen almost every day in my practice, and I wouldn't pretend to take credit for them. There is a greater force working unseen among us, of that I am completely sure. It took me almost thirty years to find and describe it, but of course by now we both know just what that is... *The Undying Soul.*

Chapter Fourteen

⌒

CARTER: THE SOUL REVEALED

THE PLEAS OF MY PATIENTS trapped in the modern world—between ancient faith and scientific atheism, kept reminding me that they felt abandoned, confused and fearful of what lay ahead in the vast unknown they were approaching. When I began my search for a more effective and loving way to help them transition from this world to the next, I had no idea what I was looking for. This much I did know:

Something terribly vital was missing.

Until I discovered what that *something* was, my patients would remain ever-fearful facing the void…and I would spend my career stupidly standing around, helplessly watching them die.

Finally…

…I knew I had to be utterly open to whatever answers might be revealed to me. These things I knew. But the last factor—that openness?

I believed I was. *And I was wrong.* Blinded by my own intellectualism, it would take decades for me to process what I was seeing, and to fathom its meaning.

Decades.

The angel-patients I have introduced you to thus far finally convinced me to look for that *something*, as much by their astonishingly
graceful deaths as through their equally astonishing recoveries. They
were leading me, step by step, along a path to acceptance of what I had
been as-yet unable or unwilling to see.

The path to understanding and enlightenment, however, is never
a straight road. Over the years I was led toward many dead ends, only
to find myself forced back to where I started, ever-more frustrated and
confused. As I said earlier, my rational mind has always made it difficult
for me to accept anything mystical.

And let me be frank: along this journey of discovery I often wondered if the destination was itself merely a grand delusion. At times I
fell victim to self-doubt: how could I, a country doctor and certainly no
great mystic, hope to uncover and refute some hidden flaw in all that
is rational, scientific and existential? If I did succeed—if ever I thought
I'd succeeded—would I have the emotional *fortitude* to use my insights
to guide dying patients through their spiritual difficulties?

So I took stock, fortifying myself as best I could. It eventually occurred to me that it might actually take someone just like me, fluent in
the languages of science and rationality, to bear credible witness to the
reality of the soul. I had received the proper traditional upbringing in
an ancient faith, which I then abandoned following my lofty "education" in modern, secular science, embracing its inherent agnosticism.
That made me a proper skeptic, a scientist of sorts....and a physician
determined to search for ways to relieve the angst and sadness of my
mortally ill patients. That unique combination of traditional upbringing, scientific education, and many years as an oncologist produced
the meditative synergy required to make my discovery.

I thought I could trust my background and experience. More than that, I had to trust my motivation, which it seemed to me I could not escape.

All these were necessary components for a search, but by themselves not quite enough. I realized there was something else, something… dangerous, almost as desperate as the loneliness some of my patients endured: I had to be willing to challenge my dedication to scientific principles which themselves demanded that I deny any other possibilities—I had to challenge my embrace of "rational" presumptions which were in fact just as dogmatic as anything preached from a pulpit.

And if it came to it…*I had to be willing to see with my own eyes, however reluctantly, the failure of my scientific "faith" that had wholly replaced my ancient faith.*

When I first heard my patients ask me "Where is God?" the question made me ask myself, "What's missing—for them, for me, for all of us?"

False trails, dead ends, frustration…Finally, I saw *something*, first with Pavel, then with Patricia and then Clarence, Maria and others. But after each of these epiphanies, I was overwhelmed by skepticism, a skepticism that did finally recede to a whimper over time. As I have described in my interactions with Pavel and Patricia in particular, the experience was one of rapture. But then after each of them, my life went back to its daily labors and the commonplace struggles of my other patients. Even such stunning events as these can lose their effect over time if not reaffirmed, especially for a hardhead like me. These experiences were indeed "other-worldly," and in such cases it's easy to entertain doubt. Put simply, how does one hold on tight to the mystical, especially if one is by nature and profession so grounded in the empirical? That's where the frustration came in.

My times with Pavel and Patricia were five years apart, and in between I was left to my own devices, some of which included dismissing the rapture as fantasy, or worse yet, delusion. I realize now that the time in between was necessary for many reasons, the most important of which was the opportunity to re-examine in my little spare time the basic science argument in favor of the atheism that I had embraced in college. I never would have challenged these concepts otherwise. And to my surprise and wonderment, advances in basic science during the twenty-five years since my college conversion to atheism demonstrated to me that the scientific argument in favor of atheism was no longer tenable.

And it was this intellectual, *scientific* realization that was necessary to liberate me from my skepticism and in turn embrace the truth of the raptures I had experienced. I have touched briefly on these rather academic concepts in chapter nine, and will add to them in this chapter, but a more in-depth exposition is really beyond the scope of this book. The main point is that I needed time to reconcile faith and science, before I could go any further in my search. When I was with Pavel I hadn't yet done this. But by the time I met Patricia I had nearly completed these studies and so I was open to seeing the mystical as not incompatible with the scientific. And when I did, I was finally made ready for the discovery I had long been seeking.

Of course, it was a patient who showed me this light. Or, sadly, who truly reflected a frightening darkness.

Carter's Contingencies

Let me begin by saying this: doctors don't always make good preachers. I hope I'm getting better at it, but for many years I was clumsy. In practice, that means I failed to offer one patient or another the certainty and comfort they were seeking.

Carter was one of these. He first described himself as a "card-carrying atheist." But as death approached he reached a state of uncertainty, or at best some reluctant belief.

That was quite a turn. When we met, he had not only declared himself convinced that God did not exist, but demanded that I affirm this assertion. "You mean you're *not* an atheist, Doc? But you're an educated man. Don't tell me you believe in all that religious nonsense? Look at evolution, Doc. You're descended from a fish. How can you have a soul if your ancestors are tuna?"

Now it's not my practice to debate evolutionary biology with my patients. But when Carter insisted I engage him on his (pseudo) rational approach to atheism, I began to suspect he was indirectly "asking" me to help him reconcile a classic quandary of faith.

It was not necessarily my place to talk about science and faith with a patient. But there was something else, a fact of life Carter only suspected but I knew for certain: he was about to face difficult weeks of chemo, weeks turning to months and longer, only to die a harsh death from his cancer. He would need *something* to get himself through to his end.

Given that, I felt I had little choice but to venture carefully into this realm.

I wish I could do justice to Carter's cleverness. But my memories of his wit faded near the end, subsumed by sorrow, horror and regret. I cannot do justice to our conversations, so what follows here is a distilled version of my side, couched in the kind of language I'm afraid it sounded like to him. Please understand that when I address him as "friend," it's genuine. We did become friends at some time in our relationship, which only made things harder.

"I don't dispute the basic facts of evolution," I said to him at one point. "I just don't interpret those facts in such a way as to disprove God's existence, as you and so many academic biologists choose to do. For example, you make the common mistake of misusing the word 'ancestor,' a word that only applies to our human lineage. When the biologic species *Homo sapiens* came into existence some quarter million years ago, those primitive creatures themselves weren't yet human.

It likely took about 200,000 years—possibly more—to evolve a brain big enough to perform rational thought. And it is rational thought that alone distinguishes our species from the rest of the animal kingdom—the capacity to recognize moral behavior, and the will to *choose* right from wrong. A killer whale knows nothing about morality when it eats a furry seal; neither does a male grizzly, when it finds and eats its own cub. God gave to mankind alone the ability to consider the consequences of our actions, and the ability to choose to act according to moral principles.

"That means we 'descended' from more primitive species about one hundred million years after sharing a remote biologic origin with some vertebrate that *also* evolved into albacore tuna. So what?

"The point is, we have nothing *moral* in common with our predecessors, much less the common denominator of *sentience*. All brains are made mostly of proteins, so just think of it this way, my friend. The fact that the bio-molecules in Dad's sperm and Mom's egg originated in meatballs and anchovies doesn't make me a pizza pie!

"But this does raise the one theological question that has gone unanswered for 3000 years. When God imbued his creature *Homo sapiens* with free will some time in prehistory, He gave them the ability to act in violation of His own wishes. In doing so, however—by giving man and woman free will, thus a soul—did He not surrender His own omnipotence? For how can God be omnipotent if people can willfully defy Him?"

(Many theologians have struggled with this apparently irresolvable dilemma, and I refer the reader in particular to the writings of Thomas Aquinas and C. S. Lewis for a thoughtful analysis.)

"The short answer goes like this, 'God *allows* humans to exercise free will, even if their actions aren't always in accordance with His wishes. In so doing God remains omnipotent because He remains totally in control…but that then raises the even more difficult question of theodicy (the question of why God allows evil in His world).'"

It so happens that I had wondered about that last seeming paradox for a long time. So had Carter, it turned out, although to him it only offered more evidence for atheism. But we enjoyed discussing the implications of this, and lots more, during his many office visits. As it turns out, my conversations with Carter allowed me to gain a unique and compelling insight to the theological dilemma between free will and Almighty omnipotence. Bear with me if you will, and I'll offer an answer shortly as Carter's story unfolds.

Over time, Carter even relaxed his absolutism. He began to allow a "what if" approach to the existence of God, and to make allowances for such a contingency. I started to imagine that if he ever did decide to pray, his appeals would resemble those used to mock agnostics, "Dear God, if there is a God, help me to get to Heaven, if there is a Heaven..."

Certainly Carter's wasn't a real conversion. But coming from the direction he did, this effort at least gave Carter some small sense of control. By allowing for the possibility of God, at least he could bargain, which for him sounded like this: "Keep the cancer away, God, and *then* I'll believe in you."

At the time I thought that was something. Or perhaps I just hoped it helped. But Carter's offer to barter did not empty him of ego for the sake of his spirit. True faith—*sustaining faith*—requires wholeness, I've discovered, and is bled out by contingency.

This is what I tried to explain in Chapter Nine in abstract terms. Carter's story transforms those abstractions into reality, which is why his story is so important.

As you've guessed by now, Carter's offer to bargain with God failed. Fourteen months after our first meeting, we sat down in the exam room together to review his latest chest X-ray. A new spot in his lung proved the cancer was growing back. We would fight to control this relapse as best we could, but the prognosis was bleak. There was no longer a "long term" to consider. I estimated that chemo could hold off the end for maybe four to six months.

We began a new round of chemotherapy, and had some initial good luck. Carter kept his cool and hung in there for a good four months more. Then the cancer broke through with a vengeance. It spread throughout his body.

By then his body could not tolerate more treatments. Maybe he had four *weeks* left, maybe six. After that it would be "all over except for the crying," as the saying goes. And my job would be transformed from oncologist to end-of-life comforter.

Carter and I had bonded, so he wanted me to know that he didn't blame me for his relapse. He insisted that he didn't hold me guilty for "God's failure to save me." But he was still bitter.

"I'm not sure I really believed anyway," he insisted. "I asked God as nicely as I could to spare me from this, and He didn't listen. What kind of God is that anyway, Doc? Now I'm going to die, slowly and painfully. If that's how your God works, who needs Him? To hell with all that religious talk! I should have stayed an atheist! At least I wouldn't be so disappointed."

Nor would he be comforted, I would discover. Not by God, nor science. And—God help us—not by me.

For Phillip, for Benjamin and for so many others—it's not the physical pain that makes death so difficult. We relieve that pretty well with our narcotics and other remedies. The problem is spiritual, prompted by the terrible conflict of holding on to contingencies. In death, one is called to return to wholeness, to God, and in wholeness there can be no contingency. In cancer's final act, the soul emerges to take center stage. When the ego is called upon to acknowledge the wholeness of the undying soul, that ego must at last relinquish all contingencies. *This* is what Pavel and Patricia were demonstrating to me in their peaceful passings.

But when the ego resists, turmoil erupts.

"God-dammit, I don't want to let go!" Carter cursed aloud that last night, as I visited his room during my evening rounds.

At least he was being honest. As he lay on his deathbed I could see in his eyes that he was caught in a tug-of-war between his soul and his ego.

And it is the role of the ego in that tug-of-war that Carter brought home to me. As death beckoned him home, I saw something familiar in the denial that stripped him of spiritual solace.

Death is a beckoning...the final journey of the undying soul on Earth before it returns to its Source. This was something I never fully realized before my time with Carter. As life ebbs away, the *ego* no longer serves a purpose. In the peaceful deaths of Pavel and Patricia, the ego was subsumed and just faded away without conflict. In such slow and "wholesome" transitions one can visualize—imagine on a mystical level while observing within the physical realm—how the undying soul freely emerges and, unfettered from the confines of the body, is fully revealed.

But for Carter, as for many of us, ego had dominated soul for a lifetime. It had the grip of a vice rusted shut, clamped tight upon his psyche unto his last breath and heartbeat.

Maybe you've watched such a death yourself, and observed how sad and demoralizing this can be. Perhaps you didn't understand *why* it was demoralizing. I wondered myself all those years, until Carter revealed the secret when he faced death *directly*...while utterly alone.

As already described, most of my patients die while morphine floods their veins and soaks their brains. They lie in a peaceful stupor, almost euphoric, still partially able to express love and affection. They are mostly, or completely, free of pain.

Carter refused this path—and a doctor cannot force it upon anyone. He did not want to let go. He would not take any drugs that he feared would weaken his rational mind—his ego-grip.

That left him wracked with pain. He writhed upon the bed, gasping for air as the cancer filled his lungs. With each hacking breath his heaving chest stretched and scraped the internal tumors raw.

It was a brutal sight. Finally the nurses couldn't take it anymore. Carter wouldn't let them give him morphine, so he just got worse and worse. That's when they called me in: to reason with him and try to talk him into taking a painkiller.

I found Carter clutching the bedrails, sitting halfway up in bed. His face was red and covered in a musty sweat; his chest worked like a bellows, trying to capture air. Weeks of "cancer anorexia" had left him looking like a concentration camp prisoner. And this might as well have been a prison scenario, because that's what Carter was: a hostage to his ego. It had him by the throat, choking his lungs, and would not release him to death even as the cancer would not let him live. His eyes were wild with agitation, like a frightened beast—his terror as primitive as any manifest by the "ancestors" he had once claimed.

Suddenly I wondered if he'd been waiting for me. And so it was indeed. Now down to his last breaths—a cancer-ridden body can't take such exertion for long—he fixed his tormented gaze on mine, took my hand in his and spoke between fitful heaves.

"I'm not…gonna…let…go…I'm…not gonna let go…I'm not… gonna…gonna…gonna…"

Then, all at once, he did. He let go—of everything, falling back hard in the bed, emptying his lungs with one last exhale, releasing my fingers that had turned blue from his grasp. Last of all, Carter's angry, agitated eyes went dark

Instantly his room fell from chaos into a ghostly silence. In all my years as a doctor I had rarely seen anything so dramatic. Even so, I found myself ready, somehow, to understand what I'd witnessed. It had taken me almost an entire lifetime to reach this epiphany.

Here is what I realized in that moment:

Death is not an end, it is a *beckoning*. A beckoning from God to return.

That was the answer to the question Carter and I had debated, wondering if God sacrificed His omnipotence so that humans could exercise free will.

Carter's death—that moment—finally taught me the meaning of all those sad deaths I had witnessed during my career, something undiscoverable by science alone, the culmination of my quest. It took me almost three decades to see what was always there before me, but for all those years I was blind. As one of my spiritual mentors told me, "you have to believe it in order to see it."

Carter's death revealed to me that *during our lives* God *Himself* occupies our bodies with *His* soul, which we refer to as *"ours."*

And at death…each of us returns "our" soul back to Him.

We spend our lives so enhanced by this portion of God's essence that we experience choice, the chance to exercise the free will that arises from our capacity to reason and comprehend. That is what happened to *Homo sapiens* some 5 to 30 millennia ago, which is what made us *human*. *That* is why humans are not like the other animals. But we are also biologic entities, and our most powerful organ is our brain. Our brains are "owned and operated" by our egos, without which we couldn't survive.

The ego is not the soul. It is a "biologic emergent" from our complex brains. Ego is organic in the same way as are our bones and blood and belly. Like all our other organic constituents, it has a role to play in self-preservation. It keeps us from walking off cliffs or driving without headlights. It is the great organizer of the behavior of so complex a creature. But the ego has no higher spiritual aspirations than do the kidneys. Both are necessary to keep us alive, but that's all they do.

You might say that the soul is along for the ride, enjoying the physical experience firsthand, having transcended the spiritual-material divide once it occupies the body of *Homo sapiens.* For the soul to *influence* the physical realm however, it must do so in cooperation with the ego, because the ego is the *operator* of physical behavior.

Conversely, the ego has to acknowledge the existence of the soul and conform to its directives. That's been the entire purpose of religion for all time: *to inform the ego to obey the soul.*

The Common Disconnect

When the ego refuses to conform, it smothers the soul's access to the material world. The soul and its influences are thus concealed. As long as the individual remains alive, the soul lies hidden. The only way the soul can finally escape the ego's confinement is in death. And in a gradual death, like the particularly slow death inflicted by cancer, this transition can be apprehended.

In Carter's eyes I clearly saw the great tug-of-war between his dying ego and his soon-to-be released-soul. When Carter "let go," his soul escaped, and his ego, a function of the organism, was dead.

Where did his soul go? Back to where it was beckoned. Once we die, the soul "returns." That timeless and misguided contingency, "whither salvation?" must be forever discarded. *All* souls go to Heaven…to God. There's nowhere else for them to go, because they aren't separate from God. They are a part of Him, and that is what I mean by "wholeness." This *wholeness of man/soul/God* removes all the contingencies that preoccupy us, the most profound of which has always been, "Will I get to Heaven?"

I have no doubt about all of this, mystical as it may seem, because I literally *saw* that fierce physical struggle between Carter's ego and his soul there at the moment of their separation. Carter's body died. Carter's *Undying Soul* lives on. And at the very moment that I witnessed the end of that duel my psyche was simultaneously and quite unconsciously consumed with the image of Pavel lying peacefully in his deathbed, his soul and ego peacefully coexisting. The two images contrasted within me almost to the point of upheaval, until a crystallization of the message delivered by the two contrasting images appeared in my mind.

That's when I realized....

This was my discovery...

...The one I had begun searching for twenty-five years earlier.

And it was only because Pavel had come and shown me the unity of ego and soul in his overpoweringly complete way that I was able to fully comprehend that unity by contrasting it with the ego-soul division of my friend Carter. There, in that moment of Carter's difficult death, I understood at last—fully, concretely, without equivocation—the real existence of *The Undying Soul.*

Carter's soul is with God where it belongs, where all souls go. I am convinced of that, and thankful. Yet I cannot help thinking how much better it would have been for him, how his death would have been gentler, had he understood this as death approached. Carter's ego-driven contingencies, like all contingencies, led only to falsity and incompleteness. That falsity is rescued only by wholeness, the wholeness that exists as I have witnessed it, between *The Undying Soul* and God himself.

Born at one with God, we die the same way.
A dominant ego hides the soul.
Let go of your ego.
Listen to your soul.
Your own soul will guide you to the light.

Chapter Fifteen

~

LYLE: THE UNDYING SOUL

THE JOURNEY THAT IS THIS BOOK is nearly finished. Still there is one more story left to tell. After my experience with Lyle, my journey and my discovery were complete.

I began this book by introducing tragic cases, from a time in my life when I served patients only as a *physician*, because I was not yet accomplished as a *healer*. In those days I saw myself as a humanist and "post-modern" warrior, saving lives sometimes, hoping to rescue the helpless and alleviate untold miseries. Even so, I was spiritually bereft. My awakening was agonizingly slow. I learned that dying patients needed and wanted more: it took Pavel, Patricia, Clarence and Maria to convince me that there *was* more, somewhere. Through them I grew in awareness, compassion and spiritual insight, oh-so-reluctantly shedding the blinders of pride and intellect.

In short, my patients were my teachers, my spiritual guides in the search.

That certainly describes Lyle. My relationship with him was as powerful and rewarding as those that developed with the other saintly patients I have told you about. Put simply, I loved this man, as he did me.

A local woodsman and lumberjack, Lyle came to me with acute leukemia. We fought against it together for more than three years. During that period I must have seen him at least 200 times. I visited him daily during the several months he spent hospitalized in those three years. Between hospitalizations, he was in my office almost weekly.

As you saw in the story of Maria, the struggle against acute leukemia is the worst of all. Each chemo session requires a grueling month's "residence" in the hospital. Even when remission is achieved, it doesn't always last.

Lyle had four relapses and four remissions before his sturdy body finally gave in. I'll tell you about those passionate years, but it's his death I really need to share with you.

Getting to Know Lyle

Early in our relationship I was sort of spellbound, like a kid awed by an older sibling. Lyle was a ruddy old Scotsman with a weather-beaten pink face and bushy gray eyebrows. His world of toil in the woods is something many of us white-collars secretly dream about. I saw him as Paul Bunyan, Daniel Boone and Meriwether Lewis all rolled into one. And I witnessed his fortitude and grit many mornings in the hospital, watching him grin and whistle through his rough-and-tumble rounds of chemotherapy.

Lyle was the one who endured the rigorous treatments, but he was always more concerned about me than himself. Speaking with the ringing assurance of a preacher, he was eager to reassure me that he was tough enough to take the treatment. "You know, Doc, we used to camp out in an old school bus. Sometimes it was twenty below outside, so it was nice to get in there and get warm together by the wood-burning stove. Yeah, I know something about hardship so don't you worry about me," he said. "You go ahead and give me your chemo, do your best to keep me alive and not too sick, and we'll get along just fine."

That was pure Lyle. And so was this:

"Mornin' Doc," he'd holler. "How are you this fine day? Yeah, I had a rough night with the chemo but I got over it. Thanks for ordering that extra nausea medicine at two this mornin'! Hope you got some sleep after the nurses were done calling ya about me."

Honestly, that's an awfully cheery tone for somebody enduring such a brutal treatment. And I couldn't figure out how Lyle did it, until one day he told me his secret.

"Ya know, Doc, I wasn't always so level-headed. I was a wild young Scotsman, you betcha, but then I finally got over it. Do you want to know how?"

Always eager to listen and learn from him, I nodded.

"It's sort of a sad story, Doc, but with an uplifting ending. You know I have three daughters. But what I haven't mentioned is that I once had a son."

He paused. Then, for the first and only time, I saw him show a trace of sadness. His lip quivered as he went on. "My son honored me by fol-lowing in my footsteps. In fact, Bobby got to be foreman of the whole logging crew, side-by-side with me on all those days in the bush, when we worked together to bring home the timber...

"To make a long story short, well...One day a pile of heaped up logs let loose on him as he was trying to tie it down. Bobby was on the downhill side and I was uphill on top. Damned if...them logs just crushed him, Doc. There was nothin' we could do.

"We got his crumpled broken body down off that mountain and home...and for the next three days all I could do was sit and stare in silence, not sayin' a word. Honestly, I don't know if I ate or drank or if I even moved. My wife, God bless her, knew to leave me alone, until it was time to bury my boy.

"Somehow I got cleaned up, got dressed and went and attended the ceremony. I guess I was still in shock, a wonderin' how the good Lord could do this to Bobby, and to me. 'Show me a sign, Lord,' I said silently.

"After the services, I went home, collapsed and slept for a time, about eighteen hours. That's when I had a dream. And in that dream the Lord came to me. He told me…that the next time I went into the woods… He wanted me to look toward a familiar eastern hilltop.

"I didn't know what to expect. I wasn't a prayin' or church-goin' man. I was a two-fisted, whiskey-drinking Highlander. I'd always had faith in the Lord, though up 'til then I never felt I needed Him.

"I hadn't felt up to workin' just then. I wasn't ready until about a week later. But because of the dream, I found the strength to return to the work I love. I knew Bobby wouldn't have wanted me to quit. So I finally went back out there with the crew, cutting, sawing and piling like always.

"We started at dawn and broke for coffee about nine. The truck was parked in a clearing, and I sat myself in the cab as always, opening the thermos for my coffee break. I found myself staring out to the east, towards a hilltop I knew well, just as the sun broke over the treetops. Want to know what I saw, Doc?"

I was hanging on his every word, hardly breathing. The tragedy seemed *so* great, one that I myself might possibly not have been able to survive.

"You might not believe this," he continued, "but the Lord *did* send me a sign, just like He promised me in that dream. As I looked out toward that hilltop that morning I saw…the most incredible halo, Doc, surrounding the entire peak." He paused. "A halo! There's nothing natural that could have looked like that. It was bright yellow-orange… shimmering…just like you see on those old holy cards. It stayed there for at least fifteen minutes, then faded out as the sun got higher, spreading out into the sky. I sat and stared for another half hour, I guess, my mouth hanging open the whole darn time. Then I bowed my head and whispered, 'Thank you, Lord.' And right then, for the first time since Bobby died…I cried. I sat there alone in my truck and just howled out all my pain and grief. Yes I did. I don't know how long, but long enough for me to release all of my sorrow."

Lyle collected himself. He even managed a small grin. "Since that day, Doc? I haven't had a drop of whiskey or a cigarette. Fifteen years ago now. I just figured, well, if the Lord was going to go to all that trouble, He must have a reason. I figured at the very least He didn't want me wasting my time, money and dignity on booze and tobacco. You know what I mean? Sure you do...but I'm tellin' ya, Doc, it moved me in a way I can't describe...That halo, His special sign to me, made me humble and gave me purpose...so I just left my bad habits behind."

I wondered for some time about all this that Lyle told me. And perhaps you can see why, for me, Lyle was a saint like Pavel and Patricia. But unlike Pavel, he wasn't an exotic foreigner. And unlike Patricia he wasn't a Mother Teresa type. Yet in the same way, my experience with him changed the world for me as I knew it, and revealed the final step toward my discovery. He was just a regular guy of his time and place, a northwest lumberjack, whose own life changing experience gave me an even deeper insight into the wonders and power of faith.

And even more unlike Pavel and Patricia, both of whom I knew for about a year, Lyle was a part of my life for much longer...over three years! We talked often and at length—about fishing and hunting, camping, drinking, fighting, fatherhood and marriage.

But what was especially interesting was how openly Lyle talked about death—his death. Just like *he* encouraged *me* when he was having nausea at two in the morning, Lyle consoled *me* when *he* was dying. While I found that role reversal ironic, he took this mission seriously.

"You know I'm just not afraid to die, Doc," he would say reassuringly. "Not at all. Haven't been for all these years since Bobby passed."

And he wasn't. Believe me. I live with death and the dying. I see fear every day, even in people who are bravely attempting to hide it. Lyle truly was not afraid. And I know this was one of the reasons we were able to enjoy our time together.

But there was more to Lyle's mission, as I would eventually discover. How much more, I couldn't then imagine. But it was no less than him taking me all the way to my final destination in my discovery of the undying soul.

There's something special and strange about leukemia: how the body itself seems so intact. That's because all the major organs remain whole even as the disease starves them of blood, killing them from the inside out.

That's how it goes if there's even one relapse, with no exceptions—not even Lyle. He didn't expect to live forever, even though he did fight his way through four tough relapses. But he was fully intent on accomplishing one last task.

A Cabin In The Woods

About a year and a half after we met, as Lyle was enjoying a long initial remission from his leukemia, he invited me to his mountain retreat in southern Alberta. He'd purchased fifty acres of mountain property with 200 yards of waterfront along some nameless alpine lake at the foot of the Canadian Rockies. There he'd built a small cabin, and it was easy to see why his wife and daughters seldom traveled up there with him. There was a sink with running water that you could pump up with a hydrant handle; that and a drafty outhouse were the limits of its "modern conveniences."

If the cabin itself was plain, the setting was breathtaking. The lake was clear, deep and cold blue, full of char and grayling fish that we delighted in catching each evening for our supper. The terrain surrounding the lake was steep, rocky, exposed and windswept, so that even in July I had to think about exposure and be ready to make my escape to the warmth of the cabin. The less hearty would've called it desolate, but to me it conjured up visions of the entry to Heaven. The lake surface was usually active with whitecaps, and one could get soaked with spray just standing by the rocky shore. But every evening when the wind settled down, the fish came to the surface to feed. I'd catch ten, maybe twenty, in the 40 minutes of calm before darkness sent me up the scree to the cabin with the two fish I'd kept for dinner. To me the place was paradise, and I regret having made only one trip there, but it was rare that I could take an entire week off from my practice to romp around the mountains with a friend.

Lyle seemed to delight more in watching me fish than in fishing himself. It's always been funny to me that when I camp, fish or hunt with patients, they can't get over the fact that I'm more than a white-collar office guy.

Anyone who's ever been camping knows that one of the best parts of the day is the evening chow down and the time spent afterwards around the campfire. Fresh mountain air and a full day of alpine exertion always stir up a ravenous appetite, and camp food itself defines "hearty": steak, biscuits, gravy, corn, fresh trout, beer, taters…and that's just for starters. There's something special about the contentment of oh-so-satisfyingly tired muscles restored by such hearty grub, while one is safely enclosed in the warmth and security of a blazing fire and a sturdy cabin.

It is during such times that plain men become philosophers, eager to open their hearts and souls to conversation. For thousands of years men have gathered around fire, in mountain caves, on shorelines, in deserts and in meadows, conjuring up words of wisdom while gazing into flames. It's a ritual every outdoorsman delights in, first as a child listening to adults stepping out of their usual, mundane character, then as an adolescent where one first catches the whimsy and wisdom of fire-side philosophizing. Then finally on entering into adulthood, one goes on nodding at the best moments and grinning a little when the best goes over the top, as the dialogue reaches for the mysteries of the dark night sky, as if chasing the flames ascending from the crackling blaze.

Between us, Lyle and I had indulged countless years in such behavior; we were seasoned at the art of the "fiery-log banter." Even so, what Lyle mused upon, as we sat staring and talking in the typical campfire trance, left me spellbound and amazed.

"Ya know, Doc, I always believed in God and the sanctity of the human soul, ever since my parents taught me about them when I was a young 'un. But as I've said before, I didn't care much about these notions until Bobby died. From that day onward I began to think about it all more and more. And when you spend twelve hours a day workin' in the woods, you got plenty of time to think. Want to know what I've come up with after all these years of ponderin'?"

Boy, did I.

"Well Doc, it seems to me that everyone goes thru life givin' lip service to God and the soul, just like I did. But without some brutal awakening like mine, maybe that's just as far as it goes. And you know, I've talked to a lot of your other patients in the chemo room about it. I know that some of them have told you that having cancer was the source of their own awakening. That would make a lot of sense, eh Doc?"

Of course he was dead on. Hanging on his every word, I nodded in affirmation as he continued…

"Yeah, well, so I guess what I'm tellin' ya is this: Bobby's death fifteen years ago woke me up, so getting cancer hasn't had any impact on my perspective about God, the soul, or life and death. What I'm trying to say is that once you have an awakening, whether it's from being diagnosed with cancer or some other personal tragedy, it's much easier to figure out what matters most in this life, and forget about all the lesser things that keep us busy—stuff like money, career, status, or some sports team winning something that leads to pandemonium in the streets, like somebody just won a war or somethin'.

"The truth is, all that's just crap...It's nothin' compared to the truthful reality of God, and the soul He instilled in us. Ain't nothin', but even so, most of us don't get past that junk. We live in the world so worried about the daily goin's-on until we lose sight of God himself, and then we lose sight of our souls. So it all just flip-flops. The most important part of life gets lost. Wouldn't you agree to that, Doc?"

Again I quietly nodded and urged him on.

"All right then, Doc. So the way I see it is that each of us has a soul that we forget about in our daily lives. We work, we play, we eat, we sleep, we love, we fight, we win, we lose. And all that time the person winning or losing, working or playing, is doing so as a separate person, satisfying some want or ambition. Sure we got to eat and make a living, at least our bodies have to, but not so much our souls. If we were less concerned with our personal selves, and identified more with our souls, we'd probably live very different lives."

He paused and looked at me intensely, as if trying to gauge my unspoken reaction. Apparently satisfied, he continued: "I know it sounds way out there Doc, but these are the kind of thoughts you have when you've been 'awakened.' The shame of it is that often a guy's gotta go through some real tragedy to get in touch with these ideas. Anyway, what I'm tryin' to tell you in my woodsman kind of way is that over the years, as I've pondered alone in the woods on these notions, I've come to a kind of special conclusion that I'd like to share with you now—if you don't mind."

"*Pray* continue," I said grinning, pun intended.

He grinned back hugely, from ear to ear..."Hey, that's *funny* Doc, you're just a real witty SOB. Okay then, as I was sayin', the way I see it, we're all a combination of body and soul, just like we was always taught in Sunday school. That much most people of *any* faith could agree on." As he spoke I ran through my mental checklist, and concluded he was right: Christian, Jew, Muslim all hold this belief, at least in the broadest sense. So do most Eastern faiths for that matter, such as Hinduism and Buddhism. "Omigod!" I thought to myself, "the lumberjack has just sketched out the universal element from all forms of organized religion and spiritual practices!" I was definitely ready to hear more.

For a moment I thought about interrupting Lyle and launching into a discussion of the history of duality, body vs. soul, and how many modern academicians had been campaigning to do away with this "antiquated" concept. But I kept my mouth shut. The fireside is *not* the place for over-intellectualizing, as was my habit. It's the time and place for homespun truths and reaching for the magical-mystical.

"So far, all I've done is describe old-fashioned religious teaching," Lyle continued. "What-all I am saying is not new. It's what's already been said for over two thousand years: that the more worldly our lives become and the more physical stuff we care about, the bigger the gap becomes that divides these two parts of our own selves. Body and soul become separate from each other, so much so that a person even forgets that the soul exists. We lose touch with our spiritual side, which of course is our soul. It takes tragedy, or our own impending death, to shake us back to our spiritual roots. And that's just a shame…"

That's where he stopped. My patient and friend had delivered his message and left it to me to think it through. As the heat and soothing rhythm of the fire, in combination with full bellies and exhausted bodies brought on their nighttime tranquility, we found our way to our bunks, and slept a deep and untroubled sleep.

In my sleep I must have processed what Lyle talked about. Sharply focused on what he'd said, I spent the next few days meditating on it, taking advantage of the solitude, open space and grandeur available to anyone who spends time alone in the Canadian Rockies. Lyle had solidified for me what I'd been searching for throughout my long spiritual journey. What my patients needed, indeed what we all need, is to reunite our worldly personas, our "egos," with our everlasting souls.

When we are able to do that, then cancer, and death itself, no longer seem so fearsome.

The Lesson of the Wolves

On our way back home from Alberta, Lyle and I stopped at a wolf sanctuary. Some dedicated soul had put together 100 acres of prime North Idaho forest and meadow to keep two dozen of these magnificent creatures fenced off from "civilization." At the roadside office and display center he kept three young male wolves in a pen for visitors to admire. I was fascinated. I'm a dog lover, and couldn't help whistling and cooing at the huge canines. Yet they just stared right through me, seemingly oblivious to my presence. The owner came up behind me and said, "They're not dogs, you know, and they won't respond to you like a domesticated canine. They're wild, and they don't need you. I have to remind all my visitors of this interesting if peculiar fact."

Boy, it felt strange, the way those wolves just stared right through me. I wondered if they were in a trance or something. But then another visitor approached the pen with his dog, which was on a leash. Holy cow! Those wolves erupted savagely at the intruder, snarling and barking as if they were quite ready to rip the poor little dog to shreds. The terrified pooch squealed and frantically pulled his owner away from the pen. All the detachment the wolves had on display disappeared in a flash, which showed that they weren't detached at all, but rather, were highly selective in what interested them.

Seeing how startled I was, Lyle winked at me. "Those wolves don't have any problem uniting body and spirit," he said. "They just don't allow any useless distractions, like gawking tourists, to distract their attention. No wonder Native Americans revered them so highly."

Lyle's wife accompanied him on most of his office visits. They seemed very close, and I wondered why Lyle put so much time and energy into *our* friendship, and especially my enlightenment. When I asked him, he explained, "It's not that she won't listen to me, it's more that she doesn't have to. She has a solid, native faith. You on the other hand are a scientist and seek *verification*. So I'm kind'a thinkin' that as my doctor you will be the one who's going to be there at the time of my death, and so if anything special might somehow just happen, you'll be a *professional* witness to it all."

Lyle had no way of knowing what I'd seen at Pavel's death, since I had never discussed it with him. By now it had been eight years since that night of rapture when Pavel passed. Over those years I wondered if anything close to that remarkable display of spirit could or would ever be repeated. Although I had trained myself to see traces of Pavel's grace in my subsequent dying patients, painkillers and delirium almost always clouded the picture. Lyle was my first patient since Patricia and Pavel who I thought might be able to die without the usual moribund course. Now I found myself wondering if I might really witness such a glorious death one more time.

Lyle's Death

I didn't have long to wait. "I'm done with the chemo Doc," Lyle told me one day in his no-nonsense way. "My time is coming; let me be." I knew he was right, both medically and spiritually. I was actually astounded at how long he held out. His unshakable constitution kept him alive for far longer than any others I'd treated for his type of cancer.

Not long after Lyle decided he'd had enough of the chemo, his body began to wear down dramatically. We did have about six good weeks before he went to the hospital for his final stay. But by then he was too depleted to die at home. Like Pavel's, such a death is often difficult, so that round-the-clock, intensive nursing care is required to guarantee proper comfort.

Even though Lyle was quite ill, he remained strangely calm, almost serene.

"Nothin' to worry about Doc, you'll see," he reassured me. "Piece o'cake."

Well, despite his accepting attitude, I was quite upset. It wasn't easy for me to watch my dear friend finally head to the grave. Once again, Lyle reversed our roles. "Remember what I kept telling you when we were at the cabin?" he said. "I've tried for fifteen years, since the death of my son, to not lose track of my soul. You know *me*; my personality *and* my soul, right?"

I nodded.

"Well, Doc, the person you know as Lyle will soon be dead and gone. But I'm gonna give you a small present when I go. I'm gonna hang on and let you see my soul even after my body has faded out. If I can do this right, and I hope I can, you'll see something as clear and divine as what I saw that day when that miraculous halo came up over the eastern hilltop."

Then he took my hand in his, and looking at me solemnly with his preacher-like certainty, added, "If I pull it off, tell the world what you saw. You tell 'em, son."

Losing Another "Angel"

Thinking back now, I remember regarding Lyle as another guiding angel like Pavel and Patricia before him. But this interacting with "visiting angels" is not as simple as it might seem. Pavel's death had been so straightforward that I was able to understand what was happening without words spoken between us. I was also far less evolved spiritually.

So here was Lyle, about to make what I thought would be the same effortless transition. As I sat at his bedside, awaiting the coming celestial apparition, I naively expected Lyle to just repeat the display that Pavel exhibited in passing from this world to the next…

That's when all hell broke loose…

Suddenly, Lyle began to convulse. Choking, gasping—his face turned beet red and his eyes rolled halfway back up into their sockets. Frantically, I called the nurses in with the "crash cart." Speedily I did what my training had prepared me to do: I established an airway, rolled him onto his side, and ordered the appropriate anticonvulsants to be injected into his bloodstream. I held him in this safe position for the half a minute it would take for the meds to reach his brain and subdue the hyperactivity in his cerebral cortex that was causing the convulsion. Lyle then relaxed into what we refer to as a "post-ictal" state, which means he was in a minor coma, and that his heightened neuronal discharges were now controlled by the neuro-suppressant medications.

In laymen's terms, he was "unresponsive." As I reviewed his chart, I had to conclude that a seizure in this setting could only mean that he was "septic," meaning he had blood poisoning. His immune system was shot. The bacteria racing through his circulatory system would soon consume him.

I knew I'd never see Lyle conscious again.

I left his room more deflated than the fire-consumed Hindenburg, and for some reason the famous images of the explosive collapse of that noble "airship" raced through my mind. Meantime Lyle lay on his back in a heap, gurgling in delirium, burning with fever, gazing open-eyed at the ceiling, but without consciousness. I tried to console myself, "C'mon now, Steve, calm now. This isn't unusual. Dying patients often 'crash and burn' like this. That's why you wanted him here, so he wouldn't have to go through all this at home. You were lucky enough to know and befriend Lyle. What a guy! Just try to remember all he tried to teach you…"

The pep-talk wasn't working. I was falling apart.

I just could not let it end this way. I dashed back to Lyle's room and closed the door firmly behind me. I fell onto his bed and embraced him, then began to wail in sadness and grief. His body was as hot as a stove, his face and chest drenched in sweat and saliva. My tears mingled with his perspiration. Yes, this was "messy" all right.

My emotions finally drained, I pulled away and sat next to him, but his countenance didn't change. He just stared at the ceiling. I checked his racing pulse: 180! Wow! He clearly would not last much longer like this.

I sat back, staring at the same ceiling on which Lyle's unseeing eyes were focused, and waited for the end. Gradually, his breathing grew softer, less labored. Minutes before he'd been huffing and puffing. I decided to check his pulse again. It was down to 80, and his skin was much cooler. I just held onto his wrist, monitoring his pulse, which slowly but steadily drifted down: 70, then 60, then 50, then 40. As the pulse rate declined, so did the pulse pressure, becoming "thready" and weak.

Deep in his death throes, Lyle suddenly twisted about in the bed one last time. Somehow—I still have no idea what otherworldly force gave his almost-dead body the power to do this—he had turned completely over in my direction on his side, and was staring directly at me.

At first, I took no special notice, preoccupied by my sad thoughts about losing Lyle. Then my highly attuned medical intuition kicked in and forced me to pay attention. To my amazement, Lyle's gaze wasn't the same blank, empty stare of just a few moments before. He was pulling out of it, or so it seemed, while his heart rate continued to slow. Now it was 30 and becoming irregular. He was literally "inches from death," as the expression goes.

There was nothing more I could do for him medically, so I just looked at Lyle. As our eyes met, I saw something I'd never seen before, or since. His eyes were clear, as clear and alert as a live, awake normal person, not dull or cloudy or "dead."

Still, there was no outward reaction to me.

What I saw in those friendly, so-familiar hazel eyes reminded me of "eternity." It was as if he was looking deeply into me. Likewise, I could see clear into him, deeper than words can describe, into some mystical black hole that came out somewhere on the other side of the universe. All at once, in that unforgettable moment, I knew what this all meant. Lyle had died. The ego of "Lyle," my logger buddy, my woodsman friend, was extinguished, although the body on the bed was still technically alive. In other words, the "Lyle" persona I knew was not *who*, or *what*, was now looking back at his buddy Doctor Steve. Lyle was gone, yet Lyle's soul remained in the room with me. And Lyle's gazing soul wasn't looking for my persona or ego…it was looking for *my* soul.

It was the exact same eerie feeling I'd experienced when Lyle and I had gone to that wolf sanctuary, and that great spirit-creature, so focused and present, had looked not at me but *through* me, to the heart of its world.

For that timeless moment, I felt Lyle's soul touch mine. The mystical gaze of his *Undying Soul* penetrated my ego and made it all the way to my core. What he must have felt when he saw the rainbow halo on the mountain was what I then felt for the first time, in every cell in my body: the soul's presence in me, the Godly essence that exists above and beyond my own willful ego. The experience was an amplification of the earlier inklings I had received when I witnessed Pavel's passing. And in those ten years or so I had grown, spiritually, so that the full impact of the illumination of *The Undying Soul* was something I had finally become ready to receive. And this time, I had no doubts or second guesses about what had happened, nor what my duty was to bring this discovery to the light of human awareness.

Epilogue

⌒

WHAT I SAW—
WHAT IT MEANT

To be very clear about this, I will just plainly state that my extraordinary perceptions, "visions" and emotions described in this book, beginning with Pavel and ending with Lyle, were *subjective*…that is to say they were *intensely personal,* deeply moving, powerfully life-changing and illuminating.

These experiences were, in a word…mystical.

I feel I have to introduce the use of this word with some caution and explanation because some readers might be unfamiliar with its meaning, and others might object to its usage in the *context* of doctoring. But as all readers surely know by now, cancer medicine, especially as I have learned to practice it, is not just about stethoscopes, lab reports and PET scans. What I did *see* and *feel*, with Pavel and Patricia and Lyle, was not the kind of visible or emotional experience that is readily reproducible or demonstrable…in scientific terms, these phenomena were not *objective*. Which is why the *context* itself was so terribly crucial. While mystical experience has been a part of the human condition from the beginning of time, well described by sages, academicians and common people alike, sympathy toward and acceptance of such accounts is much diminished in this modern scientific age of "concrete" knowledge.

This is why this last conversation I have with you is absolutely vital. For without it, one might just dismiss the entire book and its implications as so much fantasy.

Context is the key component in virtually every kind of life-changing incident. Consider these other examples of extraordinary experience that have the power and impact to dramatically alter one's perception: falling in love, having a child, climbing a mountain peak, streaking down an alpine slope in deep powder, watching a bull shark eighty feet deep on a dive...the *feelings* those overpowering experiences generate are likewise not something reproducible on a video, or repeatable in simulation or inducible by vivid description. You can't climb to 28,000 feet or sit still in a sunken wreck watching a bull shark swim right in front of you or make your way down a black diamond slope in deep powder, until you've spent years or even decades preparing for the event. The power you feel is not accessible in a museum or on a guided tour. Those utterly moving occurrences are only open to those who spend the required time and energy preparing for the time and place, the context of the event. Which is why in fact many participants in these types of exhilarating endeavors often do refer to them as mystical, or at least bordering on such.

But all these types of adventures, however daunting to attempt, *can* be realized by those committed to the task. And no one would deny that the adventures are real, or assert that the exhilaration and expanded-awareness quality is just fantasy.

Similarly, the love of a partner, or a newborn child, so absolutely and positively real, is *not objective*. And yet, no one would deny that that love is real! All the while there is no recipe for these experiences, because they are profoundly contextual...and intensely personal.

Maybe…just maybe, the mystical is more real and more common than we think. Maybe we have as a culture lost touch with it, when it has actually been a commonplace throughout human history. Maybe… just maybe, the fantasy is in believing only in the concretely real, a belief system that is itself so fantastical that it logically reduces into such conundrums as "dark matter," and "parallel universes."

Mystical experiences have been described throughout the millennia. Some have been unintended, especially within the context of a sudden intensely personal event, such as the death of a loved one or even upon a walk alone in a spring garden at dawn.

It has been argued by some that participating in a life-changing transcendental type experience *usually* requires many years of preparation, usually in the form of discipline, such as meditation, fasting, or prayer. In that *context*, one can more confidently "ascend the mountain" to that higher spiritual plane; it's not unlike what it takes to get to the peak of Everest. It's not easy. Nor quick. Nor typically accessible to the undisciplined.

That's how it had to happen for me. It took decades, working day and night, always searching, and even then only occurred via the peculiar visitations into my life of Pavel, Patricia and Lyle. I do not believe these were simply random or fortuitous encounters. My passion for the quest intersected with their angelic *intent*, which combined to create the particularly unique *context* in which my own stubbornness and pride could eventually be overcome. My epiphany could only unfold after years of preparation, which finally resulted in the bending of my very unyielding ego to the sublime truth that they took great pains to reveal to me.

Personally I make no exclusive claim to these insights and their mystical realm. However, I do voice a caution to those who may want to replicate the journey. I pray that you do in fact embark…but I also beg that you spend the time and devotion required to create the context in which you yourself may be personally successful. I want others to follow where I've been. It has in fact been quite lonely on this journey at times. But as the pathfinder, I don't want those who follow to be gasping in the thin air or to disappear in a crevasse.

You've come this far, and my primary purpose has been to bring these truths to light for all to see. They are of so much less use merely kept to myself…and are otherwise only revealed to those souls already passed. So let me propose a next phase of discovery, far more important than any solitary quest. I passionately encourage all readers to embark on their own personal expedition whose goal is to allow you to *see* for yourself. To empower you to *feel* for yourself, what I have seen and felt. After all, what could possibly be more important than addressing the questions raised here? Why settle for a life less fulfilled? What I have seen and felt is real! Now decide to make it real for yourself! Disregard the cynics and the atheists. Embrace your own power to recapture your spiritual birthright and enter the mystical realm. Make plans to embark on your own exhilarating ascent, so that you too can look out from the top of the world…

Along the way, don't be afraid or deterred if you happen to stumble and fall. That's almost unavoidable. Just do all you can to make the proper preparations and, most especially, create your own context. Be sure to be ready to accept your own spiritual guides when they do appear. It will be very difficult to stay on the path without them. And if perchance you find that you might need or want my assistance at some challenging place on the journey, just let me know. I'll always be ready and willing to lend you a hand ... and you know where to find me ...

Know this then, as I finally know it now: cancer may be one mysterious force that devours the material body and evaporates each individual ego. But it does not destroy the greatest part of our being. That most important part is what emerges when the material body has become so torn and tattered that it can no longer contain the precious, the priceless…

…The Undying Soul.